# Praise

'Sophie Milliken oozes ambition and is a highly driven businesswoman. In *The Ambition Accelerator*, she shares her pearls of wisdom and the blueprint to success that has taken her recruitment business from zero to hero. As the winner of Best Business Women in Recruitment 2019, it was Sophie's tenacity and creativity that impressed the judges. In this book, she shares her experience and knowledge openly and honestly, conveying how she has made a significant mark in the recruitment world.'
— Debbie Gilbert, Judge, Best Business Women Awards

'As a student in my final year of university, I found *The Ambition Accelerator* to be the perfect guide for me. Sophie provides amazing, real-life advice not only on your career path, but on handling the tough moments in life, too, and how there are always positive outcomes from these times. She also includes success stories from other powerful women, which are truly inspiring. This is a must-read for women of all ages.'
— Georgina Bulga, final-year student, University of Liverpool

# THE
# AMBITION
# ACCELERATOR

The working woman's guide to powering up
your professional success

## SOPHIE MILLIKEN

# R<sup>e</sup>think

First published in Great Britain in 2021
by Rethink Press (www.rethinkpress.com)

Cover image © Freepik.com

*To my daughter, Jessica. You inspire me daily with your enthusiasm and excitement for life. I can't wait to see what you choose to do with it. Whatever you decide, so long as you are happy, I am happy.*

*And to my BBs, there is no other group of women I would rather celebrate or commiserate with. You are all very special.*

# Contents

# Foreword

So often we can find ourselves 'stuck', whether this is personally or professionally. The 2020 pandemic made many of us re-evaluate the way we work and left us faced with different challenges as well as different possibilities. I myself had to take a step back and work out ways to ensure my business not only survived but thrived in this new world. Taking those steps in 'pivoting' and adapting has felt risky, scary and at times overwhelming. But with a strong network of incredible women (and men) around me, I have been supported and encouraged. Seeking advice, asking for help and checking in has allowed me to make more informed and considered decisions than if I were to try and go it alone. The importance of having a strong network to support us has never been so evident. These networks look different for everyone – they may be made up of colleagues, business connections, friends or family. Whoever it is, it is never too late to start networking to ensure that when you fall on tough times, there are people around you to pick you up, dust you off and cheer you on.

Being curious and resourceful has helped me to level up and accelerate my own career, as learning from others' experiences has allowed me to seize opportunities as well as identify the importance of giving back. Operating my business with a 'pay it forward' mentality at its heart enables more thoughtful decision making and reinforces community ties, which are so important. I am always learning and have been inspired by Sophie ever since I met her three years ago. Having already written a bestselling book on career advice for graduates, Sophie is well equipped to offer practical and actionable guidance to those who wish to power up professionally. This book will enable you to have courage in your convictions and give you more confidence to take a seat at the table.

Sophie's own career trajectory has perhaps not been straightforward, but it has evidently taught her so much. Lucky for us, she has taken the time to share these lessons in this book, highlighting the importance of resilience, hard work and getting back up again. Through both personal and professional (what seemed like at the time) setbacks, she has demonstrated that things don't always turn out how you might have planned but these times will always teach you something, leading you down a whole new path that you may never have foreseen. Through this book you will be given the tools to take the next step in reaching your potential and hitting those goals.

Whatever stage of your career you are at, it is vital to keep learning. For those who are looking for a digestible and relatable guide to kickstart their career, this book is for you. By offering practical exercises as well as tips and tricks from hugely successful industry professionals, *The Ambition Accelerator* promises to empower you to identify key areas of growth and create a mindset that will help you fulfil your potential.

The need for adaptability and a strong network may seem obvious; however, with Sophie's help you can put these things into practice without feeling overwhelmed by the tasks ahead. She leads by example and writes with humility, admitting her own missteps while helping you, the reader, to learn from her mistakes. Her emphasis on collaboration and listening to her employees, while rewarding them for the big wins and protecting them from the losses, shows why she has enjoyed such fantastic career success as a leader of her own business. I personally have gained a huge amount from this book, and Sophie shows that through true grit and determination, you can power up your professional success.

**Simone Roche MBE**
Founder, Northern Power Women, Northern Power Futures and the Power Platform

# Introduction

As I made my way to the big red circle in the middle of the grand stage of Birmingham's Royal Conservatoire, I was shaking with nerves. I was about to give my first TEDx Talk in front of hundreds of people, and the talk had the power to be seen by many more. I felt sick.

Dressed in my long gold dress and wearing my Jimmy Choos, I oozed confidence. But what the audience didn't see was the sheer panic I had felt during the tech rehearsal the night before. The rehearsal where I was so bad that my colleague and friend Rachael told the organiser, 'OK, that was bad, really bad. Don't worry, she will pull it out of the bag tomorrow.'

I stumbled over my words, my tone was unnatural, and I couldn't remember what I wanted to say.

I had been dreading and looking forward to this talk in equal measures. I was given special permission to bring my eight-year-old daughter, Jessica, along to the event and I wanted to make her proud. I returned to the hotel feeling deflated and unbelievably overwhelmed. I spent the rest of the night practising, cutting bits out and trying to get into my stride. Rachael kindly offered to have Jessica sleep in her room that evening so I could rest and made me practise my talk before I went to sleep.

'Do slide one. Right, now do it again. Now again, but include slide two.' Rachael's coaching was intense, but it helped. By the morning I was feeling slightly more confident. We were given access to a dressing room a few hours before my talk was scheduled, and we spent that time going over the talk again and again. An hour or so before I was scheduled to give the real talk, something major shifted. I started sounding more relaxed, and I was even ad-libbing. I began to realise I was ready to do this. Just as well, as time had run out!

My TEDx Talk was called *The Truth Behind the Showreel*.[1] I was lucky to have been approached to

---

1    S Milliken, *The Truth Behind the Showreel* [TEDx Talk], 2020, www.youtube.com/watch?v=woZ_d3WTtR4, accessed 16 September 2020

deliver it by one of the organisers. Although I was nervous, it sounded like a great opportunity, so I said yes. It was also a scary opportunity, but I think the best opportunities often are the scariest. Initially I was going to talk about something completely different; I can't even remember what now, but it was something loosely related to my business: supporting graduates to secure the job of their dreams.

In the run-up to my TEDx, the speakers had three meetings. At the first meeting, my contact, Lesley, tried to coach me on my topic. She put down her paperwork at one point, looked me right in the eye and said, 'Where do you get your grit from, Sophie? What is it that makes you so driven? That's the story I want to hear.' So I started to talk. I spoke about how I came to set up a business following a corporate career with a major department store group, about becoming a wife and mother and then later a divorced and broke single parent, and about how that motivated me to improve my situation. 'That's it,' Lesley said. 'That's your story. Will you share it?'

## Most of us don't know where we are going

As I shared in my TEDx Talk, my life looks glamorous, exciting and successful now. I've won multiple business awards, written a bestselling book and created a successful business. I have a wonderful group of friends and I live in a house I love with a healthy and happy child. But that didn't happen overnight. It has taken an unbelievable amount of determination and hard work. Did I always know what I wanted to be when I grew up? Not at all.

When we are young, our career aspirations are shaped by the people around us – typically our family and teachers. Almost all young children go through a phase of wanting to be a teacher or in the police force, both roles that we learn about at an early age. Over time, career advice has improved in schools. It's certainly better than when I was at school, when the art teacher was also the careers guidance person. He looked at me blankly when I told him I wanted to be a fashion buyer.

Careers guidance in schools still has a long way to go. However, in this age of fast change and rapid techno-logical developments, the crazy fact is that the job – or jobs – that you will end up doing were probably not on your radar as a young child. They might not even exist yet!

## How to use this book

The aim of *The Ambition Accelerator* is to inspire and motivate young women in the early stages of their career. I've read lots of books by women which inspired me but weren't relatable or practical. I want this book to be both of those things to you. This is your book, and you should use it in a way that suits you and your learning style. You may choose to read it in order, or you can dip in and out of the sections that are most relevant to you.

I wrote this book during the coronavirus pandemic in 2020. Like everyone else, I was stuck in the house during lockdown, and I kept waking up at 5am. I was worried about the uncertainty in the world and panicking about what it meant for the business and the people I work with. That was on top of the worry about my family's and friends' health and wellbeing. I deal with challenging times by taking a pragmatic approach, and writing gave me something to focus on during those early starts.

Initially this book was to be the backstory to a TEDx Talk I delivered in Birmingham just before lockdown. My idea evolved, and it became what you have in your hands today. *The Ambition Accelerator* is part backstory and part guidebook, supported by some hugely useful advice from successful women from a variety of backgrounds and industries. I used the lockdown as an opportunity to approach women I admire and ask them to do a video interview for this book. The incredible Simone Roche, who wrote the foreword to this book, introduced me to many of the women you will hear from. I knew some of the others from various business interactions, and with just a few I approached them and they said yes to getting involved.

I couldn't include every gem that was gifted to me during the interviews, so I have turned the video footage into a podcast series, which you will find at www.sophiemilliken.co.uk/ambition-accelerator-interviews. Definitely check it out, as I know you will be inspired by the interviewees' backstories and where life has taken them so far. The common themes among these women are:

- None of them ended up doing what they thought they wanted to do when they grew up

- Imposter syndrome has been an issue for each of them at various points in their careers

- They encourage asking questions at every stage.

- All of them value learning

- They will all inspire you

The book is split into five chapters. Chapter One covers my personal story. I started my career by taking the traditional route of completing a graduate scheme after university, before leaving the company twelve years later to set up a business. If you were to look at my LinkedIn profile or google me, your perception might be that I have 'made it'. I do have a good life, but it has taken a lot of hard work and some really tough times to get to this point, and it certainly isn't easy now. I will share some of the lessons I have learned so far.

Chapter Two looks at lifestyle, in particular the myth that is work/life balance and other important aspects of lifestyle that will influence your career progress. We often sacrifice things like sleep in our quest to progress at work, but by investing in our self-care we will actually have more energy to put into our passions.

Chapter Three focuses on building your network: from finding your tribe to the value of role models and creating your own team. Chapter Four is about harnessing your potential through the power of planning and by taking and learning from opportunities. Much of the content in this section relates to mindset and learning, both of which are vital to success in any industry.

Chapter Five brings everything together. Here, I suggest you change your path if you aren't happy, share some final advice from the women I interviewed and encourage you to be bold.

My hope is that you will finish this book feeling inspired and motivated to achieve success in your career, whether that means going down a traditional route, becoming an entrepreneur or something in between. Like the women I spoke to, I am a huge believer in seizing opportunities and taking action, so it is also my hope that you will take some of the actions suggested in this book. Whatever you do, do it with passion, determination and good intent.

# 1
# My Story – Lessons I've Learned

## The early entrepreneur

When I was a child, I loved coming up with money-making ideas. I don't know where this came from. I grew up in Newcastle in the North East of England with parents who had met at university and stayed in the area. My parents both had normal jobs: my dad was a structural engineer and my mum was a social worker. No one else in my family had ever displayed entrepreneurial tendencies. I have two younger brothers, so perhaps my fighter instinct came from having to scrap with them to get the best-looking plate at dinner time.

As a small child, I used to enlist the help of my next-door neighbour, Kate, to join me in my crazy ideas. An early idea was to buy up as many penny sweets as we could, stretch them and sell them for 2p. That was probably my favourite, although I suspect we ate more than we sold. We used to make things out of paper and sell them outside Kate's garage. Kate often reminds me of the time we sold tattoos, which involved us going to our neighbours' houses, drawing on their hands and charging them 50p for the privilege. I don't know how we got away with that one!

When I became old enough to get a part-time job, I did. I had a paper round at age thirteen, which was my first taste of having my own money – about £8 a week, if my memory is correct. By the time I was fifteen, I had a Saturday job earning a massive £1.88 an hour at the Wimpy in town. That was hard work. Doing a deep clean on a Saturday morning following the indiscretions of Friday night revellers is not something I miss. The free lunch was decent, though.

Once I finished school, I went to university because it was expected. My parents had gone, so it was just assumed that I would go. Looking back, I wish I had sought advice about which course to do and where to study, but at that point I decided to study retail management at Leeds Beckett University. I chose the university I went to purely because a boy I was in lust with was there, and the course fit with my aspiration at that time to be a fashion buyer.

While I was at university, I secured a part-time job at the biggest nightclub (at the time) in Leeds. I worked my way from being one of a team of eight in the cloakroom to selling tickets from the box office, before being giving a stint on the VIP bar. I *loved* that job. My wage was fairly decent for a student, and it was generously topped up by tips from the clients who frequented the bar. After a few months, I became the VIP bar supervisor and I was in my element. I got to mingle with Leeds United players (who were riding high towards the top end of the Premier League in those days), soap stars and lots of other random celebrities who were in the club for events, filming shows or just hanging out. When I finished university, I was almost sad to graduate because it meant giving up that job and heading into a career.

## Lessons learned from the corporate world

After completing my degree in Leeds, my plan was to become a fashion buyer. I thought this would be a glamorous role involving international travel and selecting nice things. When I realised it would involve living in London, I sacked that idea off. At that point, I thought London was a scary place and I was craving a move back to Newcastle. Although I wouldn't necessarily change my path, I do wish I hadn't seen London as a barrier, as it later became the catalyst that supercharged my career and, eventually, my business.

Instead, I headed back to Newcastle after university and took up the place I had been offered on a retail management graduate scheme. Despite having worked in part-time jobs since I was thirteen, starting this job was a reality check and a real introduction to the working world. I quickly learned some tips to help me adjust.

My contract hours were from 8.55am to either 5.15pm or 6pm, depending on the day. I used to arrive at 8.45am, thinking how keen I must look. Wrong! By week two, I had been pulled up by my manager to suggest that, as a graduate, I should be in by 8am to prepare for the day ahead and to show my enthusiasm. I remember feeling outraged, but it got me into what has become a really good habit. I am definitely at my most productive early in the morning, and I used to get so much done in that hour before the shop opened. Another tip someone gave me early on was never to get drunk in a work environment. I've mostly stuck to that rule, and I can look back on my career to date knowing I've never embarrassed myself on a work night out. Staying reasonably or totally sober at work events has also provided some amusing moments, as I've been able to stay fairly lucid while seeing others become worse for wear.

A friend recently told me that he felt I have always been ambitious (he's known me since I was sixteen), whereas I look back on my slow progress after graduation and feel that wasn't the case. I do remember being desperate to get each promotion in those early years, but I think that desperation actually held me back. When I became more successful in later years and took that pressure off myself, I was able to thrive more quickly and in a less stressful way.

Within five or six years of carrying out almost every junior management role in the Newcastle store, I was sent on a secondment to head office in London for six months. I sobbed for the whole of my last day in Newcastle. I knew I wouldn't be back.

## The Big Smoke

Despite my apprehension about moving to London, it was one of the best moves I ever made. I'd fallen into HR by that point and was given an exciting role designing training materials for managers in new branches. I was in my mid-twenties, living in the up-and-coming Shoreditch area of East London, enjoying my job and getting to spend time in other cities like Cambridge, Liverpool and Leicester too. At the retailer I worked for, we were always encouraged to take ownership of our self-development, and this made a huge impact on my progress in later years.

While in London, I took an opportunity to complete my master's in HR Management. This developed my knowledge and confidence and introduced me to the world outside my employer. During the course, I secured a role managing graduate recruitment for the organisation. This role was the game changer. I fell in love with that job. I joined what is now the Institute of Student Employers, started to network with other employers and universities, and spent time on campus meeting students. Every day was fun and exciting. During my five years in that role, I went from managing one graduate and one summer placement scheme to having five graduate schemes and fifteen placement schemes.

Being a member of the Institute of Student Employers led me to meet some amazing people and develop my networking skills. Some of the people I met then became clients when I set up my business, and I am still in touch with many of them today. Through both my master's study and my networking, my confidence in my own ability grew along with my love for the role.

One high point was introducing a graduate scheme in buying. My boss suggested I shadow a buyer, so off I went to Portugal on a buying trip. Lucky bugger, you might be thinking. Well, although the buyer and merchandiser I travelled with were great fun, the reality of the role was not so. We took a budget flight to Porto, hopped in a cab and went straight to a towel factory. We then spent the whole day looking at towels and talking about them. It was a long day, fuelled only by a couple of espressos. Where was the glamour I had dreamed of when I aspired to be a buyer as a student? As part of the trip, we had to go out for dinner with the towel factory owner. This was more fun, given that we went to an amazing restaurant, but then we had to spend the whole evening chatting about towels and making polite business conversation. Not so fun. It was so useful doing this trip, as I experienced the downsides of the role as well as the upsides.

Alongside this development in my career, my personal life was also changing. On a weekend trip back to Newcastle, I met the man who was to become my husband. After around two years of long-distance dating, we got engaged and I wanted to move back to Newcastle. With a heavy heart, I told my boss it was time for me to either get a regional job or leave. She stunned me by suggesting that I stay on in the role but work half of the week from Newcastle and half from London. This type of arrangement was unheard of then, but it worked well for a long time. My husband would drop me off at the station in time for me to catch the 5.25am train down to Kings Cross. If it was on time, I'd be at my desk by 9am. I'd do a long day in the office and then enjoy a night out with a friend or my brother, sleeping in their spare room before another long day in the office and a late arrival back in Newcastle on Tuesday evening. Then I would spend the rest of the week working from home or at a university campus.

With the birth of my daughter, Jessica, this routine became more challenging. So much changed for me with her arrival. Becoming a mum seemed to mean I'd been thrown back into the 1950s. My husband and I had always shared household chores equally, but there seemed to be this feeling from him, and from society, that as mum I would take on the bulk of the responsibility for Jessica and for the house. I didn't mind that to a point when I was on maternity leave (although my maternity pay was higher than my husband's take-home pay), but when I went back to work it became a real bone of contention.

I put so much pressure on myself as a mum. I wanted to be the best I could be for Jessica, so I exclusively breastfed her for as long as I could. She didn't sleep too well, and a well-meaning friend persuaded me to put her on a formula milk at night time when she was around six months old. When that didn't improve her sleeping I sobbed, thinking I was the worst mum ever.

The pressure we put on ourselves is astounding. In the run-up to returning to work, I stored up so much milk in the freezer that I was able to ensure that Jess had milk until she turned one. Every drawer was full of it, interspersed with the various purees I had blitzed up. I wasn't a natural mother, and I spent most of Jess's first year feeling worried and upset that I wasn't good enough. I went to every baby class going and read all the recommended books, desperate to learn the tricks to do well in this new role. When I look back now, I regret not just doing the best I could and enjoying the experience more. Hindsight is always a wonderful thing.

When my maternity leave came to an end, I agreed a new working arrangement with my super-flexible boss: full-time hours over four days, so every Friday off with Jess. Sounds great? It was, mostly, but two of those days were in London and the mum guilt was raging. The childcare rota fell to me to sort out, and it was a mix of childminder, nursery and my mum for a couple of years.

## A new opportunity

While I was on maternity leave, an organisational change was announced for the whole HR function. I ended up going back to work earlier than planned, as I wanted to be involved in the changes and felt that being present would give me the best chance to secure a good role. My role ended up changing so much. It was being moved to Bracknell, and I was also asked to go back to five days, spending three of those at my desk in the office. I debated moving south again but quickly discarded that idea. It was time to leave.

I looked at roles in graduate recruitment and more widely in HR in the North East. There were hardly any at the level I had been working at and nothing specifically in graduate recruitment. I was going to have to take a massive pay cut or come up with another plan.

As has happened many times since, an opportunity came to me. A chance conversation with Simon, who I had got to know through the Institute of Student Employers, led to us meeting for lunch to discuss business ideas. Simon had been working in a similar role to mine for one of the big banks and also had a crazy commute from north to south each week. He had aspirations to work for himself, and we spoke about different ideas over pizzas at Zizzi in York. At the end of the lunch I said I would be up for going into business with him – and that was that. It was a bonkers start to a business for two people who had been in steady corporate roles for years, but an exciting one too.

## Becoming a single-parent entrepreneur

Things started to fall apart with my husband when he said that he didn't have enough free time, even though he was going out with his friends a couple of times a week while I was looking after Jess. The resentment started to build, and the party-boy lifestyle became more of a problem. We grew further and further apart. The things that had attracted me to my husband – his easy-going and fun nature – became the very things driving us apart. I knew the end was coming.

## Getting stronger

Becoming a single-parent entrepreneur wasn't part of my business plan. Throughout my divorce in 2014 and for the next year or so afterwards, I had some tough times emotionally and financially. Before I set the business up, I had reached a senior level in my corporate role and I was earning a good London salary. I split up with my husband barely six months into starting the business, which was terrible timing financially. My take-home pay was around £1,500 a month, but it wasn't consistently the same amount each month. This wasn't awful for a new business, and I know many others who take nothing for years. However, my childcare costs were almost £1,000 a month. My mortgage had increased from £650 a month to around

£1,100 a month: given that I was newly self-employed, the bank wouldn't let me keep the house in my name, so my dad had to pretend he was going to work until he was seventy to go onto the mortgage with me. His age meant the mortgage term was reduced, so the monthly repayments went up.

I remember feeling trapped in so many ways at that time. Although we get on better now, my relationship with my ex-husband was difficult then. The divorce was nasty, and all of my savings were sucked up.

After an honest look at my situation, I told myself to be prepared for the next couple of years to be tough. I had to borrow almost £30,000 from my parents to pay for the divorce, keep the house and buy a cheap car. If you've seen my TEDx Talk, you will know that at the point of my divorce, I couldn't drive. It's amazing how restrictive that was, but I hated driving and had used living in London as an excuse not to persevere with lessons. By the time I was getting the divorce, the excuses had run out and my mindset changed. I rebooked my theory test (fifth time – they kept expiring) and found a driving instructor who was brilliant. Within two months I had my pass certificate. Having been learning on and off since I was seventeen, at the grand old age of thirty-four this was a big deal!

## Growing an award-winning business

I knew I was going to be broke for a while. There were no holidays or fancy things. Being able to pay the bills and not get into more debt was the goal. I re-evaluated what money meant to me. When I was younger, it was those nice but superficial things. Now, I craved the freedom and security it could offer me. Work was a godsend at that time. You will probably have gathered already that I love working, and it's always been a good escape when my personal life has been in tatters.

During my divorce, I didn't have a single day off because work had such a calming effect on me. I kept busy and worked hard because I had faith in the business. Conversely, my co-founder didn't have as much faith in the business and believed it would only ever provide well for one of us. After almost two years of discussion, he took the decision to leave and set up his own (non-competing) business. This challenging situation should have scared me and when he first made noises about leaving, it did. When he left, I was sitting in my spare room (we didn't have an office in those days) with no staff and only a few thousand pounds of confirmed work for the year. Despite this, I got excited.

My aim was to grow the business and provide security for my daughter and me. I got out on the road to speak to clients and prospects, and within six weeks I had secured around £100,000 of business. The thrill of that is indescribable. I spent time and money on self-development, which increased my confidence, knowledge and ambition. My accountant asked me how much less I was predicting we would make in revenue that year with my business partner leaving. I predicted we would make about the same as in the previous year, which surprised her. We ended up with about £20,000 more. Not a huge amount, but not too shabby none the less.

The business grew exponentially over the next couple of years. I hired staff and got an office in the centre of town. We soon outgrew the office and needed a bigger one. I won our first six-figure client, then another. We were given a place on the Scale Up business growth programme. My own profile was growing, and I was contacted by a guy called Zac who co-owned a graduate jobs board business in Manchester. We worked together on a few events and Zac floated the idea of merging the businesses, essentially by buying mine. At first, I thought this was insane, but I enjoyed working with him and his colleagues and could see the potential in doing this deal.

By this point, I was taking a decent wage and had paid off the credit card debt I had accrued after my divorce, but I had yet to pay my parents back. I was in a toxic four-year relationship, which came to an end before the deal with Zac went through. I saw the deal as an opportunity to clear my debt and give myself financial security, grow the business by joining forces with a brand in the same space, learn from people with different skills and have fun doing all this.

The year the deal happened, I had some things which seemed out of reach on the vision board I had created at the start of the year. (I'll talk more about vision boards later; I'd always been a bit dismissive of them, but when I tried them good things happened.) On my vision board there was, in no order of importance:

- Having a bestselling book

- Winning awards

- Buying a nice house in a specific area of Newcastle

- Going back to New York (that's on my list every year, best city in the world!)

- Taking a trip to a tropical island

- Having financial security

- Having the choice to send my daughter to a good private school

- Upgrading my car

- Spending quality time with family and friends

- Doing things I enjoy, such as cooking and going on spa days

- Being happy

- Falling in love

Other than the last one, every single thing happened on that list that year, and the last one happened a few months into the following year. Buying the house we now live in was an extraordinary moment. I can't tell you how much love I have for this house. It is ideally located and is just beautiful. Every time I drive up to it, I feel a huge sense of pride and happiness. Every single day, I feel grateful to live here.

Last year I published my first book and was thrilled to see it become a bestseller in a couple of categories on Amazon. Most weeks I receive messages from readers saying how it has helped them, which are amazing to read. Having the book developed my profile to the point where more opportunities seemed to flow towards me without me having to seek them out. I was offered two TEDx Talk opportunities. I won new business and was given a column in a careers magazine. We won every award the business entered that year (except one, where we were 'only' highly commended) and enjoyed some brilliant nights out with friends and colleagues to celebrate the progress and success of the business. Achieving success takes commitment, drive and determination, but I do believe it is there for the taking if you accept that it takes time and a lot of effort.

You've read a little of my story; now I'm going to take you through some things I have found relevant throughout my career and the actions I have taken. I've had the utter pleasure of interviewing a range of successful women, so you will see their views and advice throughout the chapters. Some topics will resonate more than others. Some might be topics you come back to at later points when they become more relevant. This book is yours – use it in the way that suits you.

# 2
# Lifestyle

## Work/life balance

On the day I did my TEDx Talk, there was an opportunity for the audience to talk to the speakers individually. A young woman came up to me, looking like she was about to burst into tears. 'Can I speak to you about work/life balance, please?' she asked. 'Sure, what about it?' I replied. 'Well, how do you get it?' the woman continued. I asked her how old she was and what her situation was. She was twenty-four, working for her family business and already getting anxious about not being able to balance what was important to her. I gave her the truth: 'Work/life balance doesn't exist, and anyone who says it does is talking crap.'

There's long been a view that a balance between work and life is important, for our mental health among other things. There are a few things that come into play here, though. What if, like me, you really love work? Is working a lot still detrimental to your mental health? Maybe, maybe not. If you have meaningful work, and you don't know the answer to how many hours you've worked that week, then you're probably in a happy place with it. When work doesn't feel like a chore and you've spent a week working on what needs to be done without clocking every hour, that's a beautiful thing.

The other consideration to make in relation to balancing work and life is the way we work now. People have less defined hours. We don't all work from Monday to Friday in one place of work between the hours of 9am and 5pm. Technology has enabled us to take a more flexible approach, which mostly has its advantages.

The areas discussed in relation to work and life balance tend to be family, work, health and social life (including friends and hobbies). The holy grail is meant to be a balance between them all. Having spent years trying to gain some semblance of balance, I've given up. I now realise that the best you can do is to prioritise what is important at a particular time: as Oprah Winfrey said, 'You *can* have it all. You just can't have it all at the same time.'[2]

---

2   J Mazziotta, 'How Oprah found a diet that works', *People*, 2017, https://people.com/bodies/oprah-diet-works-eat-anything-i-want, accessed 20 October 2020

When you're younger and less likely to have ties, that's probably a great time to prioritise work and social life. If you're ambitious then work hard for your employer or on your business: if you come to have ties as you get older, you will find it more challenging to do the extra hours and weekends or to travel for work.

My focus has looked a little like this over the years:

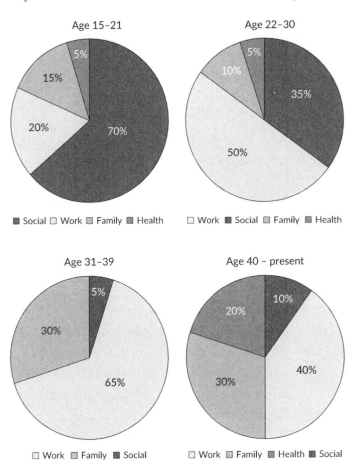

I was a real party animal as soon as I discovered alcohol, and between the ages of seventeen and twenty I probably had three or four big nights out each week – sometimes more. I always had a part-time job that I took seriously, so work was always a feature, but it wasn't a career until I left university.

As a fresh graduate I certainly prioritised work and social activities. I used to go out with my friends a few nights a week and had the stamina to do that even if I was going to be at work the next day. I didn't think about my health too much, and a cup of tea was enough to perk me up in the morning.

Work became more important when I started on my graduate scheme, but I still valued those nights out. When I got married and had my daughter, family got a bigger share of the pie, with family and work becoming the focus and only the odd outing keeping my social life going. When I got divorced, family and work were still my focus, but the family side looked a little different. I feel embarrassed that health has never been a focus, but it has definitely become more important to me in the last couple of years.

Now I have achieved many of my business goals, work is still important to me but family, health and social life have all moved up the pecking order to get more of a look-in.

**POWER UP WITH ALICE HALL**
'I did want to do meditation but couldn't get into it. I watched a spiritual leader on YouTube who said that most people are uncomfortable just sitting with themselves without their phone or the TV on, and I realised I would never sit and just look out of the window so I tried it on a holiday. I sat at the beach and looked at the sea and tried to just sit without thinking about work, and I think it had the same effect as meditation. It stops your brain from running between different themes and that helped me come down to a normal pace and then think more clearly and creatively afterwards.'

Set yourself goals linked to the elements of work/ life balance that are important to you right now. Most people know that if you write your goals down, you are more likely to achieve them. I've set business goals since 2016 and I love to smash them. In 2019 I set some family goals, which included a lot of carefully planned trips abroad. In 2020 I declared a health focus. I started walking to and from work in the new year and having walking lunches with colleagues and friends. I also took up hot yoga. In February I attended a health and wellbeing retreat in Thailand, which was unbelievably good. I planned and cooked healthy meals and I gave my supplements an overhaul.

There are loads of goal-setting templates available online, so find the one that suits you. You may want to buy a yearly planner where you set goals for the year and then follow the rest of the planner to break these down into monthly, weekly and daily milestones. It's certainly useful to get into a planning way of thinking. I've used a range of planners over the years and tried different ways of setting yearly goals depending on my theme. You can read more about planning in Chapter Four.

**POWER UP WITH MARGARET CASELY-HAYFORD CBE**

'It is very easy if you enjoy your work or if you are ambitious for your company or clients to get the work/life balance totally out of kilter. I knew things were going wrong when I kept a fridge in my office because I didn't have time to get home to have a decent meal in the evening. I learned a lesson, as I was made redundant from that job in spite of the massive amount of time I invested in it: it was a good lesson. So, it's really important to remember that you won't regret what you've invested in your family and friends and that this will buoy you up when the work environment lets you down or hurts you.

'Anyway, even if you're brilliant at your job, it's highly unlikely that you will take a totally unique skill into the workplace environment; in other words, even if you have a great qualification, you will have graduated with thousands of others nationwide with the same qualification, so the element that will make you special and interesting will be the "essence of you". The added ingredients that make you different and make clients or work colleagues relate to you will be because you have a life outside of work that gives you an added dimension.'

## POWER UP WITH LARA MORGAN

'Do what makes you happy. I've accepted that on balance, the sacrifices I have made so far give me the freedom and choice to do what the hell I bloody like, and that's a pretty good equation. Freedom and choice are the most valuable currency in the universe; there's nothing better.

'You can't do it all, have it all and be perfect. You've just got to be honest with yourself and look for contentment. I never had a balance, I was knackered. I felt like chewed string most of the time but that's enterprise, and if you don't want to play that game, you aren't going to make 20 million quid.'

## POWER UP WITH AYESHA NAYYAR

'I've got three kids. If I want to be at every single school event and home every night for homework, that's just not going to happen. You've got to accept that it's a juggling act and you are juggling many balls at the same time. Some days you win at it and other days you just have to try tomorrow.

'It's important I am a strong role model for my three girls. I want to show them you can be a good businesswoman, a good professional, good mum, good wife, good friend and a good family member. It's hard but it is possible as well. The key is prioritising what is important.'

---

**TAKE ACTION**

Get a planner. Start off gently by looking at the month or week ahead, breaking down goals and creating your daily task list.

---

# Sleep

Do not underestimate the value of sleep. Sleep is a vital indicator of overall health and wellbeing, and we need it to perform well at work. Most of us know that getting a good night's sleep is important, but too few of us actually make those eight hours between the sheets a priority.

Sleep needs vary across ages and are especially impacted by lifestyle and health. To determine how much sleep you need, it's important not only to assess where you fall on the 'sleep needs spectrum' but also to examine what lifestyle factors – such as work and stress – are affecting the quality and quantity of your sleep. To get the sleep you need, you must look at the big picture. Stimulants like coffee and energy drinks, alarm clocks, noise and light (especially the blue light from electronic devices) interfere with our natural sleep cycle.

**POWER UP WITH DAME JULIE A KENNY DBE DL**
'I was called the Maggie Thatcher of my time because I survived on four hours' sleep.'

## How much sleep do you need?

Though research cannot pinpoint an *exact* amount of sleep needed by people at different ages, most experts agree that adults should sleep for between six and nine hours. Nevertheless, it's important to pay attention to your own needs by assessing how you feel with different amounts of sleep.[3]

Try this little sleep audit now:

- Are you productive, healthy and happy on seven hours of sleep, or does it take nine hours of quality sleep to get you into high gear?

- Do you have health issues that might negatively affect your sleep, such as being overweight?

- Are you experiencing sleep problems?

- Do you depend on caffeine or energy drinks to get you through the day?

- Do you feel sleepy when driving?

---

3   'How to get to sleep' (NHS, last reviewed 2019), www.nhs.uk/live-well/sleep-and-tiredness/how-to-get-to-sleep, accessed 15 October 2020

To start a new path towards healthier sleep, assess your needs and habits. You could track how you respond to different amounts of sleep by using a Fitbit or a sleep diary. Pay careful attention to your mood, energy and health after a poor night's sleep versus a good one. Ask yourself, 'How often do I get a good night's sleep?'

To get a better sleep, try these tips:

- Stick to a sleep schedule, even at the weekends

- Practise a relaxing bedtime ritual

- Exercise daily

- Evaluate your bedroom (focusing on temperature, light and sound)

- Sleep on a comfortable mattress and good-quality pillows

- Limit your intake of caffeine and alcohol

- Turn off electronics before bed

Most importantly, make sleep a priority. You must schedule sleep like any other daily activity, so put it on your to-do list. Don't make it the thing you do only after everything else is done – stop doing other things so you get the sleep you need.

*Huffington Post* co-founder, author and business-woman Arianna Huffington calls sleep the ultimate performance enhancer. To highlight her belief in its value, she delivered a TED Talk, wrote a book and went on a major book tour. She loves sleep so much that her whole website is devoted to it. If this is an area you need to improve, take a look at the sleep resources on her website.[4]

**POWER UP WITH KATY LEESON**

'I get annoyed at myself as I'd love to be an early bird, but I just can't! I've tried every trick in the book but just can't do it. I've always loved my sleep. I'm neither an early bird, nor a night owl.'

---

**TAKE ACTION**

Do a sleep audit. Track your sleep for the next week (at least) and identify the factors that make you feel rested and those that don't. Try to incorporate the positive ones into a daily routine so that you improve the quality and amount of sleep you get.

---

## The early bird gets shit done

Are you a lark or an owl? This was the question I asked in a post on LinkedIn a while back. I had read an article in a magazine that spoke about the merits of both, encouraging us to embrace whichever one we

---

4   A Huffington, 'Sleep resources', www.ariannahuffington.com/sleep-resources, accessed 16 September 2020

are rather than try to work in a way which isn't natural to us.

I had years as an owl as a student, especially when I had my job in the nightclub, often getting home at the time I now get up. Now, I can't even imagine staying up that late. I am 100% lark and I love it. As I write this, it is just after 5am. I am sitting at the dining table in my kitchen. The house is quiet, the sun has just risen and is streaming through the bi-folding doors from the garden. The room is filled with light and calm and I have a huge mug of fresh coffee to start my day. This is my favourite time of the day. No cries of 'Mum!' expected for a good two or three hours, and fewer emails and notifications than at any other point in the day. For me, this is the best time to get a solid run at whatever I am working on.

A few years ago, I read Hal Elrod's *The Miracle Morning*.[5] Hal advocates getting up an hour earlier than you would naturally and spending that hour on a morning routine based around six key practices he calls 'life SAVERS' – silence, affirmations, visualisation, exercise, reading and scribing. You complete all the life SAVERS every morning, but you decide the relative importance of each one and apportion the hour accordingly. It's a concept that makes sense: an hour a day every week

---

5    H Elrod, *The Miracle Morning: The not-so-obvious secret guaranteed to transform your life before 8am* (Hal Elrod International, 2012)

gives you 365 hours in a year, which I reckon equates to just over forty-five additional days each year, based on an average working day of eight hours. That's forty-five days focused purely on your physical and mental health and your personal development. What could you do with that time?

I no longer stick rigidly to the miracle morning routine, but the principles have stuck with me and I use the fact that I am a naturally early riser to get up and get a head start on the day. If I have a lot on at work, I might use the time to tackle a meaty task in peace, or I might work on something that is more of a project, like writing a book.

**POWER UP WITH AYESHA NAYYAR**
'Make hay while the sun shines. I say this all the time when getting up at 5am. Nothing is guaranteed in business and all your plans can go out of the window.'

What if you are a night owl? I guess you just reverse the concept. I have so many friends and colleagues who are real night owls. I often get emails from my co-directors late at night, as that is a time when their brains are racing. They won't get a reply until the morning though, as I'm usually asleep! The point is that whatever time of day works for you, use it effectively to get stuff done. It doesn't have to be work; it just has to be valuable to you.

**POWER UP WITH STEPHANIE KAUFFMAN**

'I try to be present for my family and if I need to do work then I will go back online at 10pm. It's not for everybody but I've always been a night owl. It's important to block out time in your calendar in the morning to set out priorities for the day. Knock out some of the emails you have to deal with, then start the day fresh without any housekeeping work hanging over your head.'

---

**TAKE ACTION**

Make your own morning ritual.

**Step One: Start simple.** Pick one positive change you can make that will improve your morning routine. You might want to try elements of the 'miracle morning' approach for a few weeks and see how it works for you. Try adjusting the ratios of the SAVERS to see which gives you the most fulfilment, and incorporate more of that into your daily routine.

**Step Two: Be consistent.** You'll need to stick to your routine for a while before it becomes a habit.

**Step Three: Set your non-negotiables for the day.** Each day, write down three goals you're determined to achieve no matter what the day throws at you. These three things don't need to be chores; they could relate to your state of mind.

---

## Choose your partner well

If you remember the story of my marriage, you will know that 2014 was the year I asked my (now ex-) husband to leave. The exact date was Sunday 2 February 2014; I remember it well because it was also my mother's birthday. On the next day, I researched family lawyers and booked a meeting with the firm I had chosen. My divorce, including the financial elements and childcare arrangements, was finalised by June that year. How's that for efficient?

Later in 2014, I read Sheryl Sandberg's book, *Lean In*.[6] I was still sad about the demise of my marriage and the situation I was in, but I was also feeling more optimistic. I had worked hard on the business during this time and we were beginning to see good results. Of everything Sheryl wrote about, the advice that stuck with me is this: 'the single most important career decision that a woman makes is whether she will have a life partner and who that partner is'. Sheryl speaks about her husband Dave with such awe and love, and it comes across in the book that they had an exceptionally special and beautiful relationship. I say 'had' because sadly, Dave died suddenly in 2015.

When I was younger, I assumed I would meet my future husband at university. I didn't. I seem to have

---

6    S Sandberg, *Lean In: Women, work and the will to lead* (WH Allen, 2013)

a history with men where either they are very good-looking and fun but have a host of mental health issues or they are good, decent guys and I lose interest quickly. It took me until my late thirties to realise that neither option was ever going to provide the type of relationship I want, need and deserve.

In an early mastermind group I was involved in, one of the participants spoke about how one of her favourite things to do when she had a business problem was to work it through with her husband in the evening. They would open a bottle of wine, get a flipchart out and talk through the challenge, coming up with a great solution together. Her husband was working at a university, but he enjoyed supporting his wife and helping her work through business challenges. I recall feeling utterly jealous of this set-up and yearned for something similar. A night of drinking wine and plotting business with someone I love would be up there on my list of great evenings! It was a massive sign that the relationship I had entered about a year after my divorce was not a good one. It's interesting that from the year or so I was in that mastermind group, this throwaway story told by one of the members was the standout moment for me.

I am clearly not an expert at finding a good partner, and it is definitely with regret that I have wasted many years on men who have not been right for me. What I have learned in the last year or so has been

profound, though. There is a saying that 'the definition of insanity is doing the same thing over and over
and expecting different results', and I think that could
be said of my past relationships.

Here are some sensible traits or qualities I think anyone would agree are essential in choosing a partner
well.

## Someone who believes in you

Self-confidence and self-belief are vital to progress
in your career, but they will be almost impossible
to achieve if your partner does not fuel them. You
should want a partner who feeds your confidence and
encourages you to do anything you set your mind to.
A person willing to be in a long-term relationship with
you will show genuine support for your ambitions
and goals in life. As marriage expert Sylvia Smith
says, your potential life partner should be supportive
of your plans to advance your career or pursue a wor-
thy course.[7]

## An equal partner

When you're younger, you don't even give this issue
a second thought. Well, I certainly didn't. The reality

---

7    S Smith, '6 ways to support your spouse's career' [blog post]
     (Marriage.com, 2018), www.marriage.com/blog/tips/6-ways-to-
     support-your-spouses-career, accessed 15 September 2020

is that many men expect women to take on the bulk of the housekeeping and childcare duties. Some women enjoy this role and choose to take time off from their career to excel at home life, and that's fine. What is not fine is when both you and your partner want to have meaningful careers but don't split the home work equally. It is hard to get a fifty-fifty split all of the time, but so long as you even it out and can depend on one another when you need the split to fall a certain way, that's cool.

## Kind and thoughtful

Kindness is underrated. My mum used to tell me it was the most important quality to seek in a partner. I wish I had listened. Someone who cares and makes you their priority is huge. We often say 'treat others the way you want to be treated', which is good advice, but better advice is to treat others the way *they'd* want to be treated. In other words, your idea of what is an act of love may not be quite the same as your partner's. Little kindnesses can go a long way, yet we're often the most resistant to doing the very things that would light our partner up. Just bringing a cup of tea or offering a random act of affection can shift the entire dynamic of your day to be more loving and romantic. I love receiving flowers, but I would prefer a long walk along the coast with a brilliant chat.

A partner is not essential, but if you do have one (or want one), be sure that he or she has qualities that will help, not hinder, your career goals. My advice to anyone wanting a successful career and a successful relationship is to be clear (to yourself and to your partner) about what you need in a partnership – and don't settle for anything less. Use both your heart and your brain when choosing a life partner.

### POWER UP WITH SARA DAVIES MBE

'The importance of a good partner is off-the-chart colossal. I see this not only in my own career, as we have a lot of women in high-powered jobs in our business. Women rise through the ranks and become very successful, but then I see the pressure they get at home where they have to deal with negativity from their partner who can't cope with how successful they are and the demands that come with that.'

### POWER UP WITH LINDA PLANT

'Support is nice to have. I've worked with both of my ex-husbands and had some support. Sometimes you just don't get it at home, but you can get it from friends. Personal support is important, as it will affect your capabilities in business. We all need support; we are not islands. Be open and honest and when you need support, you can find it.'

### POWER UP WITH ALICE HALL

'I don't know where my success would have gone without my husband. I met him three months into the journey and he has always been there to listen, offer me advice and build me back up. I literally don't know how far it would have gone without him!

'Make sure your partner is a radiator and not a drain. If you go for a negative person that you have to lift up all of the time, it's not going to work. If you are going along this journey of developing your business or career and then you've got work to do around developing someone else who is always negative, that would be the worst situation. You need someone who is also ambitious and optimistic. Red flags would be people who say, "You can't do that," or, "That would take loads of work," or, "People have tried it and failed," that kind of stuff.'

### TAKE ACTION

Create a list of the qualities you are looking for in a partner. Don't make it too long and be realistic. Back in my early twenties my list would have been long and pretty superficial, with height, looks and a good job up there. I now value kindness, humour, honesty and education, mixed with that spark, of course. If your list is brief, you shouldn't compromise as it's likely to lead to tears (please trust me!) so bide your time and don't ever settle.

# 3
# Building Your Network

## Find your tribe

Work aside, who are the last seven people you spoke to? It is often said that we are the sum of the seven people we spend the most of our time with. I find this fascinating and when I first heard this, I looked at my circle and could see there were a couple of people I had outgrown, one or two who were an outright drain and then those who lifted me up.

Over the years my friendship circle has changed. Key life events meant I shed and gained new contacts. Motherhood was a major one, as was my divorce – I lost and gained a few friends at each of these milestones. When you become focused on work, as I particularly did when building the business, your tribe can become the difference between you giving it all up or smashing every goal. As comedian Amy Poehler advised in a speech to Harvard graduates, 'Find a group of people who challenge and inspire you, spend a lot of time with them, and it will change your life.'[8] This has certainly been true for me.

When I started working in the North East again in late 2013, I felt pretty lonely from a work perspective. I didn't have any friends who ran their own business; all my friends were in traditional corporate roles. I don't even think I knew anyone who worked for a small business. Everyone, including myself up to that point, had a traditional career in a large organisation, whether that was in the private or the public sector.

To meet more people in my situation, I started attending networking events in Newcastle. These events were so depressing that the saying 'male, pale and stale' could have been invented specifically for them. They were often held at times that made it difficult for a single mother to attend – early morning or early evening being the most popular. There also seemed to be a huge focus on golf: not my favourite activity. I sought out women's only events to see if they were any better, and this turned out to be a key turning

---

8    A Poehler, *Amy Poehler at Harvard College Class Day* [video], 2011,
     05:57, www.youtube.com/watch?v=T7N_L_pu74k, accessed 15
     September 2020

point for my confidence. I joined a small networking group called Forward Ladies. The group was head-quartered in Leeds but was expanding to different regions of the UK and the Newcastle group was just getting started. The launch event was packed with around a hundred women, and I left feeling so posi-tive. The group soon settled down to between ten and twenty women attending each breakfast, which was held at 9.30am rather than the typical 8am start, mak-ing it easier for those with children to attend.

After attending the Forward Ladies events for a few months, I gravitated towards a few of the women in particular, so we connected on Facebook and put together a group chat on Messenger. We were a mixed bunch with no overlap between our jobs and busi-nesses – one was in PR and marketing, one was in insurance, another was an employment lawyer, and there was an environmental consultant, a financial advisor, a specialist in powers of attorney, and me. The group chat started off as fairly professional, with us using it to ask for business advice and throw ideas about for feedback. It quickly developed into discuss-ing everything outside work too and we began to meet up in pairs, small groups and even the odd full group for a night out, which was a challenge to coor-dinate with everyone having such busy diaries.

A solid tribe of connections and friends will prove invaluable. They will encourage and motivate you when you need that and be there to celebrate the good times. Find and nurture these relationships.

### POWER UP WITH SHERRY COUTU CBE

'When I'm uncertain, my tribe is really important. Going out to our community and helping them think through things when they are uncertain and knowing that when you help others, they will also help you. Uncertainty is fine – I often solve problems by talking them through with others.'

### POWER UP WITH JACQUELINE DE ROJAS CBE

'The sisterhood in the UK tech industry is extremely strong. We connect and support each other in a very respectful and special way. I know if I have something on my mind, I have unlimited people I can go to for help. This is what sets our country apart in the tech industry. Our network is strong and we care about paying it forward to pave the way for equality and diversity in all its forms.'

---

### TAKE ACTION

Audit your contact list and keep the friends who lift you up. This can be in any area in your life, not just work. Only spend your precious time with those who energise you.

---

# Mastermind

Finding your tribe is important, but getting into a mastermind group can take that to the next level in a career context. The concept of the mastermind group was formally introduced in the early 1900s by Napoleon Hill. In his classic book *Think and Grow Rich* he wrote about the 'master mind' principle as the 'co-ordination of knowledge and effort, in a spirit of harmony, between two or more people, for the attainment of a definite purpose'.[9]

## What is a mastermind and how do they work?

A mastermind is typically between five and eight people who form a group that can meet in person or online. You can hold meetings as often as you like depending on the needs of the members but, because of the group nature, a commitment is required. Look for highly motivated people who are willing to ask for and give advice and support, and who are willing to show up for every meeting. That commitment is crucial for your success and the success of the group as a whole.

Each meeting should have a structure, as this keeps the meeting flowing productively and allows for deeper and richer brainstorming, goal-setting and account-

---

9    N Hill, *Think and Grow Rich* (The Ralston Society, 1937)

ability. In a mastermind group the agenda belongs to the group, and each person's participation is key. Your peers give you feedback, help you brainstorm new possibilities, and set up accountability structures that keep you focused and on track. You will create a community of supportive colleagues who will brainstorm together and gain tremendous insights that can improve your business and personal life. It can be said that a mastermind group is like having an objective board of directors.

I've been involved in several mastermind groups over the years. Most have been female only and one has been mixed sex. I have had different support and learned different things from each group. With single-sex groups, I've found the vibe is different. I've always gelled more with certain members who have gone on to become friends, and I share more personal information in this environment. That's just me, though – you might have a different experience, so try out a few options and see what works for you.

Whatever the make-up of your mastermind group, the beauty of it is that members raise the bar by challenging each other to create and achieve goals, brainstorm ideas, and support each other with total honesty, respect and compassion. Mastermind participants act as catalysts for growth, devil's advocates and supportive colleagues.

You will get the following benefits from setting up or joining a group:

- An instant and valuable support network

- Solutions and ideas, which come from brainstorming with the group

- The experience and skills of others

- More confidence that you've made the right decisions and are taking the right actions to achieve your goals

- Accountability and real progress in your business and personal life

- A sense of shared endeavour

- A boost to your confidence and motivation – you will feel energised after every meeting

- Motivation to achieve and exceed your goals

- The opportunity to celebrate success with the group

## Thinking of setting up your own group?

The success or failure of a mastermind group is directly related to the skill and knowledge of the facilitator. Someone who is capable of running focused meetings, holding the group accountable, and brainstorming with the members to find solutions to business challenges will enhance the group. If you are putting together your own group, you may want to take on this role and lead. Consider who you invite to the group and how many members you will have. Not everyone will be able to make every meeting: you need enough members to allow every meeting to go ahead even with a few no-shows, but not so many members that you don't then have enough time for each one.

In the groups I have been in, I find it adds an interesting dynamic to have a range of industries and backgrounds represented. You don't want to be masterminding with the competition, after all! The first group I joined was all business owners and there was variation in where we were at with our businesses. A couple of members were in their first year of trading and others had more experience. There are pros and cons to being at different stages; my steer would be not to be the person who has the most successful business. If you are that person, you'd be better off offering a mentoring service to new business owners (if you're wanting to give back) and joining a mastermind with people who are at a similar level. Having people in your group who are doing better than you is motivating. You can see where they are and aspire to reach the same level – or exceed it if you're competitive.

## The role of the facilitator

A mastermind group facilitator is the person who will run the group and take some responsibility for each member achieving their aims. As the facilitator, it's your job to set the standards that create trust and rapport, to help the members support each other, to encourage them to create effective goals and to hold them accountable for meeting these. In mastermind group meetings, the facilitator guides the group to deeper levels of examination and manages any issues that could result in conflict or threaten the unity of the members.

Give consideration to whether your group will be open to new members once it has started. If you do admit new members, it's important to make sure they'll fit into the current group and that their commitment level is equally high. Decide in advance how many members you will allow and whether empty seats will be filled. You can adopt a screening process for new members. Some questions you may wish to ask interested participants are:

- Do you have a business vision statement or career development plan?

- What goals are you currently working on?

- What is your commitment to moving forward in your career or business and your personal life?

- Why should you be selected to join our group?

If you're setting up a new group, you could use the same set of questions and use the responses to select the most committed and driven members. Even with a screening process, your group is likely to come across people who say they're committed but then don't participate, or people who break the trust of the group. Ultimately the facilitator will need to take action should any issues arise. Be prepared to ask people to leave the group if they are not participating, and do this quickly, before it impacts the mood of the other members – a slacker will bring down the energy for everyone. Having a set of guidelines or a mastermind contract that you all sign up to during the initial meeting can help keep the group on track and be used as a reminder of the commitment expected.

### POWER UP WITH MARGARET CASELY-HAYFORD CBE

'Being a member of the Casely-Hayford clan means that we had a natural masterminding group that we were born into – and it has been a brilliant motivator. It is actually open to every family to create an environment of similar mutual support (it's clearly what Boris Johnson's family has done in a big way)! One can also take the same ethos into the workplace. It's something I've always tried to do, wherever I've worked: to create a collegiate environment, so that all members feel that it's our department together against the world and we can take on all comers, and that we are better for having brainstormed a situation to deal with issues. I've

worked in organisations founded on similar principles –
like the Co-operative movement that underpins the Co-
op Group's ethos, and the employee ownership ethos
that was established by John Lewis, the founder of the
eponymous department store chain.'

---

**TAKE ACTION**

Do some research on mastermind groups and either join
an existing one or set up your own. Setting up your own
allows you to approach people you admire to join. Try to
get your first meeting in the diary in the next month.

---

# Identify role models

Do you ever think about how life would be better if
you were more like person X, Y or Z? We are often
encouraged to look to others for inspiration and while
that can sometimes make you feel inadequate, identifying role models – and, more importantly, learning
from them – can lift your aspirations and performance. Role models inspire us, and spending time
with them or reading about their success can give us
a major dose of motivation and energy. Role models
don't have to be perfect success stories. Even those
who look like they have it all can be dealing with
struggles in the background or have been through a
series of ups and downs. Those who have experienced
struggles are often the best role models, as they seem

more accessible and provide hope when times are tough.

In my corporate role, I had people in the business whom I looked up to. They were always people who had progressed well through the company and held senior positions. Looking back now, I realise I didn't know much about them other than their job title, so perhaps my admiration was somewhat misguided. Since starting my own business though, I have gained huge inspiration from role models. Especially in the early days, I specifically sought out and devoured books by strong female leaders.

The first book of this type that I read was Michelle Mone's autobiography, *My Fight to the Top*.[10] You may recognise Michelle as being famous for inventing a bra that became a bestseller. Her backstory is fascinating: beginning in near poverty in Glasgow, she details the phenomenal growth of her business. I found it intriguing to read about her innovative PR ideas and the detail of her marriage breakdown, and cheered when I read about how she slashed the tyres on her (now ex-) husband's Porsche. I once tweeted Michelle about a year into running my business after a particularly challenging day. I forget what had upset or frustrated me, but I asked her advice for an entrepreneur who was going through a tough time and

10   M Mone, *My Fight to the Top* (Bonnier, 2015)

who had taken a few knocks. She replied – and I still have the screenshot of her response – that it was normal, to dust myself off and go back to my business plan. She was right, and that advice gave me a much-needed boost on a rubbish day. Michelle gets a fair amount of grief in the press and on social media these days, often for her politics, but she will always be on my role model list.

Another book I read in the early days was Karren Brady's *Strong Woman*.[11] Karren's profile has been raised considerably in recent years by her presence as Lord Sugar's advisor on *The Apprentice,* but her own business journey is as impressive as his. One of the things that amused me about her story was that she was rejected for a part-time job at a supermarket when she was younger. The reason for the rejection was that she was 'too glamorous' and she has never shopped there since. It amused me because in the early part of my career, I was often given grief about my appearance. I remember being told off for wearing a suit that didn't match and for not wearing lipstick, so maybe I was the opposite of glamorous Karren. Joking aside, it's a good book and Karren is definitely a strong woman.

---

11   K Brady, *Strong Woman: Ambition, grit and a great pair of heels* (HarperCollins, 2012)

A book I read by an author you might not have come across is *More Balls than Most* by Lara Morgan.[12] Have you noticed a theme? All these titles refer to the strength of the women writing the books, and Lara's book is great. It relays the story of how she set up a company called Pacific Direct, which sold luxury toiletries and amenities to the hotel industry. I admire the way she treated her staff and how bold she was in securing sales for her business – the business she sold her 99% share in for £20 million. By a random twist of fate, I was recently invited to join a webinar that was being run by Lara. I got to ask her questions and we connected afterwards on social media. This led to me inviting her to contribute her pearls of wisdom to this book.

**POWER UP WITH STEPHANIE KAUFFMAN**
'My first role model was an incredible woman, Wrenda Goodwyn. One of my first jobs was at a tourism agency in Florida. I was really young and one of the first things [my boss] said to me was, "Your job is not to win Miss America," meaning be Miss Congeniality all the time. "Your job is to have a voice, to represent a point of view," she said. "People won't always like you but if you are respectful and represent your point of view with respect in tone and commitment then you are doing your job. You can't please everybody all of the time, but you have to do what is right for the business." That has always stuck with me and I still use her as a touchstone for advice.'

---

12   L Morgan, *More Balls than Most: Juggle your way to success with proven company shortcuts* (Infinite Ideas, 2011)

## Work with role models

I've gained energy from some fabulous role models who I have admired from afar and then had the opportunity to spend time with. Dr Joanna Berry is well known in the North East. I met her at a breakfast networking event where she was speaking as the cover star of the magazine hosting the event. I was blown away by her confidence and her straight talking. A few months later, an opportunity to meet her presented itself. I had gained a place on the Scale Up North East programme and was asked by my contact there about getting a mentor. It turned out that my contact knew Joanna well and asked her if she would mentor me.

At our first meeting, I felt a bit out of my depth. I actually left the meeting feeling deflated. Joanna asked about my business, which I had been running on my own for a few months by that point. I told her about the growth plans I had and how I wanted financial security for my daughter and me. Joanna didn't encourage me, which I took at the time as being unhelpful. Now I have spent more time with her, I can see that she was challenging my thinking and my focus, getting me to think more widely than about the business. I'm glad we continued to meet, as our relationship has blossomed.

Joanna is hugely supportive, and we have spent time together enjoying a good catch-up over coffee or a natter at awards bashes. A particularly proud moment was the day we both won awards in our respective categories at the FL National Awards in 2019. Joanna also spoke at the launch event for the City Ladies networking group I co-run and despite having heard some of her stories several times, I continue to be in awe of how she speaks and the challenges she has faced. She is a phenomenal speaker, and she moved many members of the audience to tears during her talk.

A great example of taking action to meet a role model takes me back a few years. I saw Nickie Gott OBE speaking at the Sage in Gateshead during an event for entrepreneurs run by one of the big banks. The event was packed, and all the speakers were impressive. This was the first time I had come across Nickie. She spoke about her business journey and was candid about her health and business challenges. I instantly warmed to her. Nickie has been on many boards and one of them was Women in the Network, which runs the biggest and best-known awards for women in business in the North East. I had entered these awards a couple of times over the years but had not been shortlisted. An opportunity to meet Nickie arose when I was invited to the launch of the awards that year. This was a great event with inspirational ladies who had won awards the previous year sharing their success stories and encouraging the audience to enter that year.

When Nickie spoke, she offered anyone in the audience the opportunity to have a coffee with her if we wanted to pick her brains about the awards and our entries. I was at the event with my friend Clare, and the first thing I said to her when Nickie had finished speaking was that I was going to take that opportunity. I hovered about afterwards to grab Nickie. She seemed a little surprised when I asked to meet her for coffee, but she was very encouraging and gave me her email address.

Later that day, I emailed Nickie to follow up. I heard nothing, so I emailed again a few weeks later. This might have been a little keen, but I'm glad I did because it turned out that Nickie had been really unwell and had only just gone back to work. Her personal assistant set up a meeting for us. I had to drive to her office in Chester-le-Street and I only had thirty minutes with Nickie. Despite leaving absolutely ages to get there, I got lost and arrived fifteen minutes late. I was mortified. I explained what had happened and told Nickie I knew she had another appointment and that I would make the most of the time we did have. Nickie relaxed me instantly and took me outside to the seating area in a big field outside her office. The first thing she told me shocked me. The reason she had been surprised when I asked to meet her was because, despite making that offer every year, not one person had ever taken her up on it. I couldn't believe it! Nickie and I sat for almost an hour drinking tea and talking about the awards and life. I took the chance to ask her questions about her career and her life. We spoke about the elusive work/life balance and how Nickie de-stressed after particularly challenging days. I loved her honesty and how resilient she was. Even now, I remember a lot of our conversation and feel it gave me a much-needed dose of inspiration.

That year, I put my award entry submission in again and was delighted to be shortlisted in two categories. The awards ceremony was glamorous and fun, but I didn't take home a trophy. The following year I applied again, and this time I was a finalist in three categories. That night, I took home two trophies, including the flagship Award for Entrepreneurship.

Nickie has had even more ups and downs with her health and business since our initial chat. I've spent more time with her and continue to be amazed by her resilience and positivity. She is a truly inspiring role model. I think one of the secrets to her success is her husband. The strong relationship, support and love they have for each other is palpable when you see them together.

Role models don't have to be famous, or even high profile. I admire things about all of the people I spend time with. I love how enthusiastic, upbeat and supportive my friend Chris is. He is known for being smiley and positive in his nature and is one of those people who everyone likes. My friend Clare is awesome. She is wise and gives great advice. She is also a massive supporter of people and I can always depend on her. She travelled all the way from Newcastle, leaving at 5am on a Saturday morning, to come and support me at my TEDx Talk in Birmingham. When I spotted her in the audience about five minutes into my talk, I was given an instant confidence boost just seeing her smile. Everyone needs a Clare in their circle.

Who is on your list of role models can ebb and flow. One person might feel relevant at a certain point in your life but become less so as your career and life move on. Keep your role model list fresh, and don't feel bad about aspiring to the successes of others.

**POWER UP WITH ALICE HALL**

'I pick up a lot of energy from people that I've worked with, people that I meet at events. With big figures, they aren't hugely accessible, although I really like Gary Vee. If I'm feeling stressed, all it takes is to watch a little Gary Vee video and I snap out of it! There's a video by him on the odds of actually being alive and it puts things into perspective. I love his content.'

---

### TAKE ACTION

Do you have a role model? How can you learn more about them or get to meet them if you haven't already? If you don't have a role model, read autobiographies of people you are interested in. They don't have to be in your field, but they do have to be inspiring. Think about who inspires you locally and look for opportunities to see them speak or be bold and ask them for a coffee. They are likely to receive similar requests from others, so make it clear why they should make time for you.

---

## Teamwork

In whatever role you go into, you will work in a team. Even if you decide to become an entrepreneur or you work as a freelancer, you will benefit from building strong relationships with the people you work with. You might have experience of working in a team in previous jobs, at school or university, or in sports or extra-curricular activities. This will probably have provided you with reflections on what works and what doesn't when collaborating with other people.

A successful organisation operates best and with the most longevity when employees work with a team mentality, each filling a needed role and fulfilling organisational goals.

Things you can do as a team to become effective are:

- **Value each role.** Everyone in the team has a role to play, so value should be assigned to each person.

- **Communicate.** You need to feel comfortable speaking to all team members. This will help you enjoy your work and be more effective as a group and, ultimately, as an organisation.

- **Get to know each other.** This is an interesting one. You won't want to become best friends with all team members and as you progress into more senior roles, there will certainly be some boundaries. Getting to know your colleagues can be done in a professional way and will help you learn about each other's strengths and weaknesses.

- **Set goals.** Whoever is leading the team should be responsible for setting overall goals, and each team member should be aware of the part they play in achieving these. If in doubt, ask!

- **Learn from failures.** Things will go wrong, and individual and collective mistakes will be made. You can always learn so much from failure and implement that learning to improve the team's future performance.

- **Celebrate successes.** When something good happens, it's so easy to move straight on to the next challenge, but success should be acknowledged and celebrated. Never underestimate the boost a team gets from celebrating.

There are plenty of tools that can help you to identify what your role is in a team. One of the simplest is the Belbin team roles.[13] Dr Meredith Belbin discovered that there are nine clusters of behaviour that can be grouped into team roles. Belbin believes that each team needs access to each of the nine Belbin team roles to become a high performing team. However, this doesn't mean that every team requires nine people: most people will have two or three Belbin team roles that they are most comfortable with, and this can change over time. Each Belbin team role has strengths and weaknesses, and each role has an equal value, even though not every role is needed all the time. By using Belbin's system, individuals have more understanding of their own strengths, which leads to more effective communication between colleagues and managers.

Belbin team roles have been around since the 1960s, but the system still works. Even if you have identified

---

13 'The nine Belbin team roles' (Belbin, no date), www.belbin.com/about/belbin-team-roles, accessed 14 September 2020

your preferred roles in the past, it is worth returning to this at future points in your career as your role evolves. There are also more complex personality questionnaires on the market now, and you might be invited to complete these as part of a development programme with your employer. Common ones include the Myers-Briggs Type Indicator (MBTI), the Strengths Deployment Inventory (SDI) and the 16 Personality Factor Questionnaire (16PF). They are all designed to help you understand your communication preferences and how you interact with others.

## POWER UP WITH STEPHANIE KAUFFMAN

'If you surround yourself with people who have shared values, you will accomplish more. I've been in groups that are mired with petty gossip, and that brings the energy down and does not allow you to be enthusiastic about your goal. I like to work with people who want to do great work and advance things. I'd rather be with folks who have shared energy and look to advance each other and create opportunities.'

## TAKE ACTION

Choose a tool to understand more about your personality and how your strengths and behaviours add value to the team. Use the results for self-reflection and to learn how to better interact with others in a team or work group.

## Build your own awesome team

One of the things I found challenging when I started out was that within only a few months of starting my job, at age twenty-two, I was given a large team to manage. Looking back, I really didn't have a clue. Almost all of my team were older than me and highly experienced in the department.

Over my first few years in my corporate role, I managed teams on various departments in the branch: sports; audio and TV; china and glass; and fashion and beauty. With the exception of some brands in fashion and beauty, I only knew a little about the products and at first this hugely impacted my credibility in the team. I recall a meeting with the HR manager where I expressed my frustration at them moving me to a new department just as I was getting to grips with the one I was in. She told me that the key to managing a team was about learning how to lead people – it has nothing to do with the product. If I nailed the people bit, I could lead any department in the store. While that doesn't apply to every organisation or management role, she was onto something. I don't completely agree with her view, but it is a fact that you are able to get your best results through your people.

When I was in my corporate role, I made loads of mistakes – as a leader and as an employee. I suffered major imposter syndrome much of the time, and I had a huge thing about always wanting the next promotion and the next pay rise. This only really changed with age and with my own business becoming successful. Suddenly, neither of those things mattered. Although I continue to make mistakes, I have learned how to bounce back from them and how to look for the positives in every situation. This makes me a laid-back leader, not in the sense of being too relaxed or complacent but in that of encouraging honesty and supporting each team member to be the best they can.

As a bit of fun, I asked my current team what they think of me as a leader. This is what they came back with:

- 'You set a clear vision but are also inclusive by encouraging us to contribute our own ideas and suggestions.'

- 'You empower us to take ownership of our respective areas and make decisions.'

- 'Visionary: you give us a clear direction for the future, always thinking of new projects, next steps – very growth focused!'

- 'Empowering: you trust us to get the job done. You encourage us to follow through on our ideas, step outside our comfort zone.'

- 'You're inspiring – your own achievements are a good example to learn from and provide encouraging boosts to accomplish team tasks.'

- 'You are straightforward! You know what you want done and make this very clear. You make assured decisions which gives the team clear direction.'

There are some clear themes that came from the team here – with lots of repetition, which I think is a good thing! I take from this that the team see me as a leader who sets a clear vision and direction, leads by example, and is encouraging and supportive of them and their work. One of the strongest things about my team is that we have an open and honest culture: something you often hear about but that is frequently just lip service. We have lively discussions and often challenge each other, but rather than causing anxiety, this is done with kindness and ultimately makes us perform better, which is something we all want.

Much research has been conducted on management and leadership over the years, and no doubt thinking will shift in the future. My advice to anyone becoming a manager for the first time or wanting to excel in their current management role is to be self-aware. You will be working with people who are all individuals, and there is no 'one size fits all' approach that will work.

There have been times when I've got things wrong with people and I'm sure I will continue to do so. All you can do is be honest, encourage honesty from your team, apologise if you have made a mistake and rectify any clangers.

## Top tips for building and leading an awesome team

### *Don't make them read your mind*

Be direct and tell your team your exact expectations. What, specifically, do you want from them? What will happen if they don't deliver? Never assume people will know what to do in any circumstance if you haven't told them, especially if they are new. Check in with them to ensure they have understood, and review progress regularly.

### *Be generous with compliments*

People like to know they're doing a good job and that their hard work is appreciated. Sometimes, all it takes is a simple compliment to keep someone engaged and willing to put in just a little more effort. If your team is killing it, you owe it to them to say thank you in whatever way you can. This can make the difference between a project being a success or a failure.

## *The buck stops with you*

If you've never been in charge of other people before, there's some bad news I have to break to you: *everything is your fault*. You might have heard of the expression 'the buck stops with you'. This means that the mistakes of your team are **your** responsibility, not **theirs**. That's why you're the leader and they're the employees. They expect you to protect them from the brunt of your client's or boss's wrath; in return, you lead them to do the right thing for the company.

## *Hire slow, fire fast*

If someone isn't working out, it's better to let them go sooner rather than later. Hanging on to a bad apple will only cause problems, not least with other team members who are pulling their own weight. You owe it to the A members of your team to manage the Bs, Cs and Ds. The goal is to have a team comprised of nothing but A-listers. That way, things will go much more smoothly, and you can focus on giving your team everything they need to be as successful as possible.

## *Celebrate success*

Every time the team achieves a significant milestone, you should celebrate. Try to do this in a way that people will value. In my teams, we have celebrated with drinks out, fancy meals, spa days, time off and parties. My current team is very motivated by food, so this is a regular feature in how we celebrate!

**POWER UP WITH LARA MORGAN**

'Don't reward somebody with something you think they want. Find out what they want and then reward them. When I finished Cranfield [University], they said I needed a BHAG so after looking that up (big hairy-assed goal) I gathered the team together and said, "Let's work out a big goal. Let's do it together, and then let's celebrate success." A smart-arse at the back said, "Why don't you take us all to Barbados?" and I said, "Well, what's the deal?" and they suggested it should be that they made a million pounds of profit. At that point, we were making about £670,000 of profit a year and within the year, we had made a million. I know for a fact all of them drank the full menu of drinks at the place we went to in Barbados, but it taught me that thing about joint rewarding and it's something we are working on in the businesses I run today.'

**TAKE ACTION**

If you are already managing a team, identify an opportunity to celebrate success in the near future. Consider what would mean the most to each member of your team and incorporate this into your celebrations. Make sure you take time to thank the team for their hard work, highlighting individual contributions.

# 4
# Harnessing Your Potential

## Personal and professional development

### As an employee

I used to hate the term 'self-development'. It was spoken about in my retail management days *a lot*. Sometimes it was a new training programme (in fairness, these were usually great) or an outdoor learning course. In my first few years, when I worked in the Newcastle branch, it was often a term used when telling me I was being moved to a new department yet again. I pretty much loved every department I was placed in, but I would just get to the point where I felt confident in managing the team and then I would be off again. It upset me at the time, but looking back, I can see the rationale.

At my corporate job, we were encouraged to always have a personal development plan in place. On the plan, we would list business and personal development objectives. These would be reviewed in one-to-ones and at appraisal time. They were linked to the annual pay review, as you would be scored in different behaviours and technical skills. As I progressed in my career, I quickly realised that if I completed the objectives within the time frame set then I would have strong evidence that I was achieving or exceeding in all areas and I would highlight this in the pay discussion. I got so good at negotiating my pay that there were a number of years when I received two pay rises in one year.

This development mindset served me well, and rather than seeing it as a pain or a chore like some of my colleagues did, I embraced the opportunities. When I had been in my head office role for a couple of years, I realised that some people were completing qualifications which were being funded by the company. I put together a proposal to complete a master's degree in HR management, identifying all the benefits this additional knowledge would bring to my department. This was approved and I began studying at London Southbank University. It was a fair commitment, with two nights a week after work in lectures and a couple of residential weekends each year. The course lasted three years and the assignments and dissertation were painful at times, but it was worth it. I met interesting people and developed my knowledge and credibility. The qualification gave me graduate Chartered Institute of Personnel and Development (CIPD) membership. CIPD membership is the badge of credibility in the world of HR. Because I also had several years in HR roles under my belt, I was able to complete a further assignment directly with the CIPD and upgrade my membership to become a Fellow.

## As an entrepreneur

When I left retail management and set up the business, I didn't have the same formal development opportunities. That didn't matter though, as setting up a business from scratch brings a whole wealth of on-the-job learning. Every day I was learning something new. I developed knowledge in accounting, marketing and systems. Some areas interested me more than others. There is a misconception that you need to always work on your weaknesses. I remember my former business partner telling me I needed to do an Excel course because I was terrible with spreadsheets. I resisted this the whole time we worked together, which I am glad of, as spreadsheets are the epitome of boring for me. My view on weaknesses is that we all have them and we can't be good at everything. If the weakness is in something that is essential then sure, work on it and improve; but if it isn't and you don't enjoy it, get someone else to do it!

In those first couple of years of setting up the business, I had been reading plenty of books. I had also managed to get us some coaching from a woman I rated from my time in my corporate role who was keen to support us as a new business. Fiona is an excellent coach and was never afraid to challenge our thinking, which I got so much from. We met with her every few months and took on board much of what she said.

When I took over the business in early 2017 after my business partner left, self-development plans came back with a vengeance. I had joined the Female Entrepreneur Association (FEA) in late 2016 having come across its founder, Carrie Green, on Facebook. This was another turning point for me. I loved Carrie's story about how she came to set up the FEA. The short version is that she set up a mobile phone unlocking business in her second year at university, despite having no knowledge of this industry. Carrie taught herself how to master Google AdWords and the business became so successful that it was making her considerably more money that she would earn as a lawyer if she completed the Legal Practice Course at the end of her law degree. Although Carrie was making lots of money, she felt isolated and, after a period of reflection, she set up the FEA to provide support for other female entrepreneurs. If you haven't come across Carrie, check out her TEDx Talk[14] or read her book, *She Means Business*.[15] She has a massive work ethic and a seriously entrepreneurial streak. The FEA got me into planning and measuring progress. I began setting myself financial targets and posting more consistently on social media.

Carrie made an exciting announcement in the FEA Facebook group one day. She was hosting the first FEA retreat later that year. I got excited. My diary at this point was rammed and she had said it was going to be in September. The busiest time for my business is in autumn, so I thought the chances I could go would be slim. By a fortunate twist of fate, when the dates came out they were the only ones I could do in September. It was also in Palma, which was a cheap flight away from Newcastle.

The retreat was just what I needed at that time. Three days in Palma with twenty women from around the world was hugely inspiring. It showed me that I was further along with my business than I had realised, and having time and space to think gave me all sorts

---

14  C Green, *Programming Your Mind for Success* [TEDx Talk], 2014 www. youtube.com/watch?v=MmfikLimeQ8, accessed 16 September 2020
15  C Green, *She Means Business: Turn your ideas into reality and become a wildly successful entrepreneur* (Hay House, 2017)

of ideas. I left with some great new contacts who have since become friends. One of the ideas I came up with while I was there cost me £40,000 to develop and was a total flop, but I have no regrets – it was valuable learning and I've been able to use elements of that idea to progress subsequent ideas.

Since going on the retreat, I've set myself development challenges each year. One year I completed my Level 7 qualification in coaching and mentoring. In 2019, I completed the Key Person of Influence business accelerator, which is run by bestselling author and serial entrepreneur Daniel Priestley. That course was another game changer. I was in a cohort of seventy super-confident businesspeople, all looking to become key people of influence in their respective industries. We met monthly for formal training and were set challenges after each session. These were mostly time-pressured but were all hugely useful for us. I was placed in an accountability group with six other people, who have become great confidantes.

## New challenges

One of the big challenges of the Key Person of Influence course was to write a book. I loved that part of the course. It was so exciting; we planned the whole of our books out in one day. I left clutching a load of coloured cards which showed the layout of my book. I'd had a great chat with the publisher who was running the day and decided I wanted to take the hybrid publishing route. I explained that I wanted to release my book that September. Because it was a book for students and graduates who wanted to get a graduate job, it needed to be available for the application window that would open that month. With it being May, I thought I had plenty of time. It turns out I had a lot to learn about publishing. No, the publisher told me, I had three weeks to complete the finished manuscript. Luckily it was a time of year when I could clear most of the diary and just focus on writing. All I did for those three weeks was write. I had the opportunity to refine it during the publishing process, but the bulk of the work was completed in that short window.

My most recent challenge was delivering my first TEDx Talk, an opportunity I was given off the back of my book. I know a few people who have completed TEDx Talks, and most of them had to apply to speak, often being rejected a few times before securing a slot. Even though this opportunity made me feel ill, I knew it was a good one and I said yes. I am not a natural public speaker, but who is? It is a skill that can be developed and in a previous year, I paid for some coaching in this area. After I said yes to the talk, weirdly three other less scary opportunities came up to speak at events. I said yes to all of those too; they served me well in preparing me for the big red circle.

My advice on self-development is that you should do it. Identify what you would benefit the most from and what you will enjoy. If you don't enjoy it, don't do it: it will be painful and it will take ages.

### POWER UP WITH LARA MORGAN

'Every time I travelled, I read a book on business. I would bend the corners of pages, rip pages out sometimes and put them in my team's boxes, ask them if they thought we should do this. That gave us cutting-edge information but not a complete plan, so I got a grant for learning and had a life-changing experience at Cranfield. Since then I've had the privilege of going to Stanford. I've even lectured at London Business School. That constant learning underpins everything. This morning I was up at 7am and listening to the Global Fit Summit because I'm trying to become an expert in fitness, health and wellness. How do I learn? I listen to the experts.'

---

### TAKE ACTION

Reflect on what you want to improve. If there are several things, you may wish to create a personal development plan with multiple objectives. Alternatively, you may wish to set one large goal, like taking a course or getting a qualification. The key thing is to do something and commit to it so that it gets done. Once you've done it, set another goal or plan.

---

# It's all in the planning

Do not underestimate the value of planning – for your business, your job, your career or your life. It might sound boring, but when you set goals and make a plan to achieve them, you are more likely to be successful. In his 2018 article for *Forbes*, Mark Murphy found that those who wrote their goals down clearly were 1.2 to 1.4 times more likely to achieve them.[16] I was surprised to read that men are slightly better than women at this, as all the planners I have ever known have been women.

**POWER UP WITH LINDA PLANT**

'I've always evolved in business. I get on to something and then I get on to the next thing. That's not to say I don't have planning. When I'm interviewing, I always tell *The Apprentice* candidates to set realistic goals. They come on and they have a business making £20,000 and next year with Lord Sugar's investment, it's going to make £1.2 million. No, it's not!'

## Goal-setting and monitoring

Goal-setting might look slightly different depending on what your chosen career path is. If you've cho-

---

16   M Murphy, 'Neuroscience explains why you need to write down your goals if you actually want to achieve them', *Forbes*, 2018, www. forbes.com/sites/markmurphy/2018/04/15/neuroscience-explains-why-you-need-to-write-down-your-goals-if-you-actually-want-to-achieve-them/#7fb528127905, accessed 20 October 2020

sen a traditional job route, then you'll probably be encouraged to set goals that are related to the organisation you work for, although good companies will also support and encourage more personal goals too. If you have gone down the entrepreneurial route, your goals will be focused on how you grow your business. Either way, setting goals is a good thing. Reviewing them regularly is essential so that you can check you are on track and adjust your plans accordingly to ensure you reach significant milestones.

Once you have a solid understanding of what you want to achieve, you can set goals and think about how you are going to work towards meeting them.

Ask yourself these questions:

### Identify

- What's important to me?

- What do I need to achieve?

- What are my strengths?

- What are my development areas?

### Plan

- What resources are available to help me?

- When do I need to achieve these goals?

- Who will support me?

## Take action and record

- What methods of learning are available?

- How will I achieve my goals?

- Who could coach or mentor me?

## Review and reflect

- What have I learned?

- What could I do differently?

- What's next?

You can record your goals, objectives and areas for development using a personal development plan. This is an action plan to help you get from where you are to where you want to be.

You can download a personal development plan at www.sophiemilliken.co.uk/the-ambition-accelerator-resources.

Reflect on outcomes and evaluate achievements and progress. Review and re-establish future plans and goals

Self-assess skills and identify strengths and weaknesses

Develop your skills, eg through workshops, online courses, seminars, self-study, conferences, mentoring, practice and more

Prioritise development needs in consultation with supervisor(s) and develop a plan of action

If a personal development plan is too formal for you, you might want to try a vision board. These are more creative and they're certainly fun to do. About five years ago I did my first one, having thought that they were a bit too fluffy for my liking. I found the process fun and put things on my board that seemed a distant dream. To my surprise, they all came true within a year and I have refreshed my board every year since. Not so fluffy after all!

## POWER UP WITH AYESHA NAYYAR

'At the start of every year, I sit down and work out what I want to achieve. So there was a turnover goal, a staff count, an efficiency, opening a new office, winning awards. The first year I won an award was a big deal. You've got to set goals. If you don't know where you're going, you might get there, but not necessarily in the quickest or fastest way. You've got to have a plan.'

## Recording your achievements

When in a job or starting your own business, you'll probably be working on many different things at once. Fast-forward a few months and you probably won't remember all your successes and achievements. If you keep track of your successes now, they'll be easier to recall when you have a performance review or set new goals.

You can download a copy of my 'record your accomplishments' worksheet at www.sophiemilliken.co.uk/the-ambition-accelerator-resources.

Although it's important to set new goals once you have achieved your current ones, it's also important to recognise your progress and celebrate success, so make sure you do that!

**POWER UP WITH STEPHANIE KAUFFMAN**
'I mapped out a two-year and a four-year plan, knowing that the goals would change and my path wouldn't always be linear. Through that process, I made sure that I really understood the business. I would raise my hand for the assignments that weren't always sexy but ones that I knew would make a difference to the business. One of these was figuring out Universal's call tree. If you called up Universal as a guest to find out information about the theme park, it wasn't the easiest of experiences. I'm not a call centre expert but by unravelling that, I made a difference and caught the chairman's eye. He realised I

could fix problems. I wanted to be one of the youngest vice presidents in a male-dominated space, not the first female VP but VP in general, regardless of gender. And I did that at thirty-one.'

## Short-term planning

Do you always have a to-do list on the go and consider yourself super-organised, or are you always wondering where the time has gone? If you aren't already, you need to become organised because this will ensure that you keep to deadlines, become more efficient and get stuff done.

As my time has become more squeezed, I've had to get more organised. I plan yearly at a high level as well as monthly, weekly and daily. This might sound excessive, but it isn't when you have a system in place that works for you. There have been periods of my life when I've ditched planning, and doing so has always caused me to become less focused and less efficient.

Even basic to-do lists will focus your day and ensure you get more done than if you just rock up to work without a clear agenda. Maybe you could try both and see the difference planning makes. There is something superbly satisfying about crossing things off that list. It's like tracking steps – when you see you are almost there, you push yourself to hit your target.

You need to find methods that work for you. I know people who only look at their emails once or twice a day and some who have someone managing their inbox and calendar. Most successful people I know plan and track their success, so that does seem to be a common theme. Work out how you want to operate and be consistent, so it has the impact you need it to. Next, I'm going to share a method that I've found to be effective.

## Bullet journaling

The bullet journal method has taken the planning world by storm. I have always had some type of list-making on the go since I started my first corporate job. Previously, it would be a notebook that started out as pristine and beautiful, using my best writing for the first page or so but becoming scrappy and ragged from then on in. More recently, I used single pieces of scrap paper, which felt good on an environmental level. I then heard people mention bullet journaling.

Initially I wasn't interested, as I thought it was journaling in the traditional sense – essentially, keeping a diary. I was so wrong! After hearing more and more about it, I decided to buy the book *The Bullet Journal Method* and find out what all the fuss was about.[17]

---

17    R Carroll, *The Bullet Journal Method: Track your past, order your present, plan your future* (Fourth Estate, 2018)

Ryder Carroll, the guy who invented the bullet journal, used to be a multiple-notebook person. Constantly behind and anxious in school and as a teenager, he was given a diagnosis of attention deficit disorder. He began to develop small journaling tricks to get through his classes; in college, he carried around six notebooks to keep track of everything. He also scrapbooked and made collages. He started writing down his thoughts in short bursts throughout the day and found that it calmed him, allowing him to see past his anxieties to their root causes.

In the years after college, Carroll took night courses in web design and worked for media companies in New York. That's when the bullet journal really started coming together as he slimmed down and organised his books. He noticed that many of his co-workers kept journals too, though they did so irregularly. In 2013, he built a website and shot a video explaining what had become his unique method. His aim was to save people the pain and time he had spent getting to this point.

The result was a set of organisational instructions. Basically, you take a journal, number the pages and create an index so you can find everything. From there, you can list tasks, write diary entries and create a calendar. Bullet journaling (or BuJo, as it is known online) has developed its own vocabulary. People identify as bullet journalists. There's a daily log, a monthly log and something called a future log. You can create symbols for notes, events and tasks, and other symbols to indicate when a task has been completed, scheduled, moved to another section or deemed irrelevant.

There are collections of related material, such as shows you want to watch or books you want to read. There are trackers for anything you feel compelled to monitor: sleep, workouts, mood or alcohol. Each day, you practise 'rapid logging' using short sentences and bulleted lists, and then each month, you review everything you wrote down and move only what is meaningful to the next month. If this is a new concept to you it might sound complicated, but once you get into it you'll discover that it really isn't. There are loads of short videos explaining it on YouTube, so take a look and see if it appeals to you. I found this method easy once I understood the various symbols, and it is a great way to keep on top of things and to note down the many thoughts I have running through my mind.

## Adapting to unexpected changes

There are always things that you can't plan for. Life might chuck a huge curveball that derails you: you could lose your job or a big contract, for example. If this happens, don't panic or think that it can't be fixed. Adapt to the new situation, consider your options and be flexible with your plan. Your goals could remain the same, but the method and timescale for achieving them might need to be tweaked. Speak to friends, family or trusted colleagues if you need help to reach your goals or advice on how to get there. Under no circumstances give up – especially if it's an important personal goal! Adapt if necessary but life is too short for regrets, so make the things that matter happen.

---

### TAKE ACTION

Set some goals. Decide whether to use a vision board or a personal development plan; it doesn't matter which, as long as you set them. Schedule a time to review them and celebrate when you smash them.

---

## Ask for help

One of the best things about starting out in your career is that there is no expectation for you to know it all. If you're a school leaver or a graduate, employers aren't hiring you for your knowledge, work experience (although having this is helpful) or strong technical skills. They are recruiting you for the potential you have shown and for your enthusiasm. Employers know that they can teach you the rest as long as you have a lot of enthusiasm and a passion to learn and progress.

One of the worst things about starting your career is that you might not know it is fine to ask lots of questions, and you may worry about appearing too needy or being a nuisance. We all know that children ask lots of questions. Perhaps you have a younger sibling and you've seen this first-hand or your parents have told you about how many questions you asked as a child. Children ask lots of questions because everything is new and they seek to understand. Starting a new job is the same, so make the most of being new and ask as many questions as you can! In his book *Intern: A doctor's initiation*, cardiologist Sandeep Jauhar recalls his first day as a newly qualified doctor at New York Hospital. Addressing the new class of interns, Dr Shelby Wood, the hospital's residency director, gave them this wise advice: 'The only mistake you can make is not asking for help.'[18]

When I set up my business, it was like being the new girl all over again. There was so much that I just didn't know about – things which seem pretty basic to me now. If I hadn't asked lots of questions, I wouldn't have progressed and I would have made unnecessary mistakes that would have cost time and money. There's a misconception that people know it all when they progress in their careers, but that is just not true. All of the women I spoke to in my research for this

18   S Jauhar, *Intern: A doctor's initiation* (Penguin, 2008)

book identified the value in asking for help, even in the most senior roles.

### POWER UP WITH SHERRY COUTU CBE

'I use social media to ask for help. It's not unusual for me to say on Facebook or Twitter, "I'm thinking about this... can you help?" and it's amazing what comes back super-fast.

'LinkedIn is a fabulous product; you should make it your friend. Sometimes I will post to LinkedIn about something we are doing and the comments we get back are super-interesting. In terms of my tribe, my go-to might be WhatsApp, and sometimes it's fellow board members chatting about a board paper we thought was terrible or we didn't understand. Social media allows you to be in tune with things. I went on a trade mission with a bunch of female CEOs about three or four years ago and every day, there are still interactions with that group we put together. Every day things are shared within that group. Social media allows you to find your tribe. Sometimes it's public with a post, sometimes it's private. They are amazing productivity tools, as you get your answer quickly, so find the tool which suits you; I tend to use them all for slightly different things.'

### POWER UP WITH LINDA PLANT

'I ask for help from respected experts. We mustn't be afraid to ask for help. Life is a learning curve and if you are ambitious and motivated then you do what it takes to get to where you want to go.'

**POWER UP WITH JACQUELINE DE ROJAS CBE**

'I found myself employed as a managing director for the first time and I was sat at a big desk and I thought if anyone asks me anything about this business, I have no idea what to say. I decided to shift my leadership style from one of "knowing things" to one of "not knowing". In other words, I adjusted my leadership style to be curiosity-led. Questions became my friend.

'Children never stop asking questions, and great leaders never stop being brilliantly and incessantly curious.'

---

**TAKE ACTION**

Who can help you now? Consider what you need to know to move towards your current goals. Contact at least one person you know who can give you some advice and help develop your knowledge.

---

# Make quick decisions

Making quick decisions is a skill that increases your productivity, gives you authority and demonstrates confidence. This is a skill that can be developed by improving your confidence and by implementing certain ways of working.

Are you a perfectionist? Do you agonise over making sure your work is the best it can be? A key lesson I have learned is that getting something done is usually better than striving for perfection. If you procrastinate, your progress will be slowed. Consider the Beatles as an example. The Beatles are often thought to be the best band of all time. They were actually active for less than eight years, but during that time they were prolific, recording 213 songs, roughly one song every twelve days.[19] Can you name all 213? Probably not – and some of them are probably not great, even if you are a major fan.

Oprah filmed 4,561 episodes of her show,[20] Albert Einstein authored over 300 papers,[21] and Richard Branson has launched around 100 ventures.[22] Too often we wait for the perfect time to do something, but that time isn't likely to come. Make the decision and get stuff done. If you've made the wrong decision, act quickly to remedy it. What's the worst that can happen? Unless you're a doctor, probably nothing too awful or so bad that it can't be rectified. In the wise words of Michelle Obama, 'You can't make decisions

---

19  B Wyman, 'All 213 Beatles songs, ranked from worst to best', *Vulture*, 2017, www.vulture.com/2017/06/all-213-beatles-songs-ranked-from-worst-to-best.html, accessed 20 October 2020

20  K Fallon, 'Oprah's last show: A recap in quotes', *The Atlantic*, 2011, www.theatlantic.com/entertainment/archive/2011/05/oprahs-last-show-a-recap-in-quotes/239483, accessed 20 October 2020

21  M Oshin, 'Einstein's most effective life hack wasn't about productivity', *Quartz*, 2018, https://qz.com/work/1494627/einstein-on-the-only-productivity-tip-youll-ever-need-to-know, accessed 20 October 2020

22  M Russell, 'Richard Branson's fails: 14 Virgin companies that went bust', *Business Insider*, 2012, www.businessinsider.com/richard-branson-fails-virgin-companies-that-went-bust-2012-4?r=US&IR=T, accessed 20 October 2020

based on fear and the possibility of what might happen.'[23]

The same thought process can usually be applied to your personal life. If you want a family, there is unlikely to be a perfect time for this to happen – and if there is, biology may not support your desire. With a baby or a house move, just get cracking if it's important to you. You will then become more resourceful in making it a success.

**POWER UP WITH ALICE HALL**
'I hit a point where I wondered how sustainable the pace was. We were at a point where our whole life was this business and we asked ourselves if we were going to have a personal life. We decided four years ago to try for a baby and it didn't feel like it was the right time, but if we didn't just do it, we never would as we were so obsessed with the business. We had our little girl and that was the first time I had no choice but to step out.'

There is a school of thought among some top leaders that by simplifying the daily choices you need to make, you will have more energy and headspace to devote to bigger, more important decisions. In turn, you'll be more productive because you won't be wasting time on things which don't really matter.

---

23  J Davis, 'Michelle Obama's life lessons to live by', *Harper's Bazaar*, 2020, www.harpersbazaar.com/uk/culture/culture-news/news/a39397/25-of-michelle-obamas-greatest-quotes, accessed 20 October 2020

High-profile examples of this in action can be seen in Facebook founder and CEO Mark Zuckerberg and former Apple CEO Steve Jobs.

In 2014, Mark Zuckerberg had his first ever public Q&A session. He answered many questions in that session, but one of the most interesting ones was, 'Why are you wearing the same t-shirt every day?' In case you haven't noticed, Mark Zuckerberg wears the same grey t-shirt at most public events. He answered with this: 'I really want to clear my life to make it so that I have to make as few decisions as possible about anything except how to best serve this community.'[24] Zuckerberg doesn't actually wear the same t-shirt; he has twenty identical grey t-shirts at home. For him, what he is wearing is really not that important. Of course, he needs to wear *something*, but he doesn't want to think about it because it doesn't fall into the 20% of the decisions he should be making. Instead, he focuses his energy on how best to serve the Facebook community and simply wears the same grey t-shirt.

Similarly, Steve Jobs famously wore the same black turtleneck, blue jeans and New Balance trainers every day. This quickly became his signature look as well as a part of the overall Apple brand. He also understood

---

24   E Kim, 'Here's the real reason Mark Zuckerberg wears the same t-shirt every day', *Business Insider*, 2014, www.businessinsider.com/mark-zuckerberg-same-t-shirt-2014-11, accessed 20 October, 2020

that he had a finite capacity of brainpower to make well-thought-out decisions.

While this behaviour could be perceived as extreme, we can apply the concept to our own lives. Ever spent ages deciding what to cook for dinner or wasted so much time deciding what to watch on Netflix that you could have seen a full show in the time spent deliberating? A bit of planning can go a long way in simplifying your life and gives you the headspace for other stuff. Consider meal-planning and scheduling. Look into bullet journaling (mentioned earlier in this chapter) for this: you could have one page on which to record recipe ideas or meal plans, and another page to write down shows you've heard about which you want to watch, or books you want to read.

This approach is sometimes called 'decision minimalism', and you may want to adopt some of the basic principles.

### Streamline your work wardrobe

Unless you're a celebrity or working in a creative industry, what you wear is not important, so it isn't worth overthinking. Keep it simple by identifying a few styles you like, so that you don't waste time each morning deliberating what to wear that day.

## *Create a morning routine*

Whatever time you rise, you should be full of energy, high in brainpower and sharp in your decision-making ability after a good night's sleep, so complete your most important tasks as soon as you can after waking. Is there one thing that you could get done that will allow you to feel like you've been productive, even if you get nothing else done for the rest of the day? This is often called 'eating the frog', and there is a great book by Brian Tracy – *Eat That Frog!* – which goes into further detail.[25]

## *Batch-cook meals*

Do some research on what to eat, find a few recipes for each meal and batch-cook them one evening or at the weekend. Use a meal planner (or your bullet journal) to plan your menu each week. This is a great way to eat well, reduce food waste and save time on deciding what to cook and eat each evening.

## *Unsubscribe from unnecessary information*

Reduce the amount of content you consume. Often, you don't need more information; you just need to act on the information you already have. The same goes

---

25  B Tracy, *Eat That Frog! Get more of the important things done* (Hodder, 2013)

for social media. Consider turning off notifications for the channels that are less relevant and useful to you. It's so easy to lose an hour looking at utter crap on social media – we all do it. But don't fall into the trap too often.

## Jot down key objectives before bed

Doing this will help empty your head ready for sleep and give you more clarity for the next day. Write down what you want to get done tomorrow (you could use a bullet journal to do this) and your notes will help form your to-do list for the next day.

### POWER UP WITH MARGARET CASELY-HAYFORD

'It's important to make a decision, when you've weighed relevant issues in the balance, and to accept that you aren't infallible and could make wrong decisions but that you shouldn't allow that thought to paralyse you. It's better to be decisive than not to make a decision at all; and to be clear in doing so, especially if you're leading a team – and if necessary, review the decision later and correct it, explain the rationale for doing so – rather than prevaricating and allowing circumstances to take over. Take soundings, listen to hear and then decide. You know what they say: people who stand in the middle of the road get run over!'

Whether you're deciding what to eat for dinner or making a choice about a project at work, you're faced with making dozens of decisions each day. Making these choices quickly can save you time and anxiety. It helps to take a step back and think about how important a decision will be in ten years. You should also figure out the main criteria or objectives you want to achieve and make decisions in line with these.

To make tough decisions quickly, it's best to aim for adequate rather than ideal – done is better than perfect, remember! You can follow a process to make better decisions as you become more confident in your own judgement. Try this one out and see how you get on:

- **Pick an option and run with it.** As long as you have eliminated the 'bad' options, pick one of the solutions and run with it. Since there is never enough time to weigh the future consequences of every little decision, simply trust your gut instinct, which is often accurate, and take action.

- **Get your team together to do a 'brain dump'.** If your work project is facing a lot of complications, you may want to get all of your team members together to problem-solve the situation. By getting all of the expertise relevant to the decision in one room, you can reduce cognitive overload and accelerate decision-making in your project.

- **Assign due dates at meetings.** Always assign clear and realistic due dates at meetings. All too often, vague due dates are set for important actions and their related decisions. Instead, take the initiative to make sure due dates are listed for all of the important actions that come out of your meeting.

- **Get over your fear by looking at the consequences of inaction.** If you are scared about the consequences of making the wrong decision, it is important to work through this fear. To do so, consider the long-term consequences of not making a decision. Once you have gained perspective on the serious consequences of inaction, go ahead and make the decision.

### POWER UP WITH SARA DAVIES MBE

'It's always effort and reward. As the business gets bigger your time is limited, and you can't always do what you want to do, so what can you do that gives the greatest return? When I was younger we did everything, but now we can't run with every idea I have, so I weigh up which will give the greatest return for the least amount of effort.'

---

### TAKE ACTION

What easy ways can you make decision-making simpler in your personal and work life? Look at the strategies in this section and pick one or two that you can implement now. Try them and review the impact after you've been using them for a few weeks.

---

## Resilience

According to the Institute of Student Employers, resilience is a key skill that employers say graduates often lack.[26] This highlights the difference in the education environment, where you are the customer, to the workplace, where you are serving the customer. If you want to progress in your career or be a successful entrepreneur, you need to increase your resilience. The great news is that this is a skill that can be developed.

The Cambridge Dictionary defines resilience as 'the ability to be happy, successful, etc. again after something difficult or bad has happened'.[27] Unfortunately, as the definition states, to gain resilience something bad or difficult has to happen – and that is not pleasant or fun. There is a way to avoid this: you can get a job that comes with very limited amounts of stress, where you go in, do the work and don't have to think about it again until you return the next day. There are plenty of jobs like that, but if you want to progress to have more responsibility and a bigger salary, you need to accept that the rewards usually come with more stress and more risk. With that in mind, developing your resilience is key.

---

26  Institute of Student Employers, 'Development Survey 2019' (ISE, 2019), https://ise.org.uk/store/viewproduct.aspx?id=14816181, accessed 15 September 2020
27  *Cambridge Dictionary*, 'Resilience', https://dictionary.cambridge.org/dictionary/english/resilience, accessed 10 September 2020

Resilience isn't about becoming hardened to life; it's about developing healthy strategies that allow you to deal with challenging situations and then progress. Being old enough to have worked through two major recessions and a global pandemic, plus a divorce and a horrendous miscarriage, I can say my resilience has been severely tested several times. One of the first times I had to show resilience in a work environment was when I applied to the M&S graduate scheme – in the year when they pulled their scheme. I had advanced all the way through to the assessment centre stage, so I was feeling pretty good. I will never know if I would have been offered a place, but when it was no longer an option I shifted my focus to the application I had ongoing with another retailer. This was an easy disappointment to bounce back from, as it didn't feel personal.

When students tell me they have been unsuccessful at interview or at an assessment centre, the first thing I ask them is if they have requested feedback. Often, they haven't, as they are still smarting from the disappointment of not getting the job. It does feel personal, so they miss the opportunity to seek that guidance about where things went wrong – valuable learning that they could apply to future job interviews.

I can recall so many examples of when learning from failure and displaying resilience felt more personal and therefore more painful. This happened a lot in my early years in retail management. One of the first challenges I had was managing teams of people who were older than me and knew a lot about the business and their department. I started on a higher salary than most of the section managers who were my new colleagues, despite their years of experience. This led to a certain level of resentment towards anyone coming in as a graduate. Looking back, some of the behaviour I experienced in those first few years would now be classed as bullying. Almost exclusively, the nasty behaviour and comments directed at me came from women.

The incident that was a turning point for me was the only challenging situation I had encountered with a man. I was told that my work was 'shit' by one of my managers. There had already been some challenging situations with my manager that I had just accepted, but it had got to the point where I was so unhappy in that role that I felt my options were either to leave or to tackle my manager's behaviour. I'm so glad I chose the latter. Often, when you find yourself in a tricky situation you imagine the worst possible scenario, so any improvement on that is a win. Looking back, the action I took was bold – I asked to have a meeting with him away from the department. I told him how I felt when he told me my work was shit and how miserable he was making my work life. I explained that I wanted to progress and learn from him but I felt like he had taken an instant dislike to me.

There was a moment when he paused, and my mind was in overdrive thinking about which way this conversation was going to go. It went the right way. He apologised and admitted he had a chip on his shoulder that I had come in as a graduate and that he was assessing me against much higher standards than any of the previous managers he had managed. He went on a course around that time which made him realise we had starkly different learning and management styles and that he needed to acknowledge and respond to my style rather than only accepting his own. This was a huge turning point, and our relationship improved so much that he remains one of my favourite people I have worked for. When I was moved into a new role a couple of months later, I was genuinely gutted. Funnily enough, a year later he had a larger role and needed a new manager for a specific project. He requested me, so we got to work together again. That role was a total joy.

I learned from that incident – and many more that have occurred since – that feeling upset, frustrated, angry or uncomfortable at work is seriously horrible, but it is unlikely to resolve itself. As with most things, taking action is the way to go. The way you go about this will have an impact on the end result, and it is important that you try to deal with these situations calmly, presenting facts and even using humour if appropriate.

**POWER UP WITH JACQUELINE DE ROJAS CBE**
'Resilience is something which makes you very independent but if you don't ask for help, you make a binary decision rather than amplifying your choices and I think that is a very important part of resilience.'

## What creates resilience?

A *Psychology Today* article describes factors that appear to make a person more resilient, such as a positive attitude, optimism, the ability to regulate emotions and the ability to see failure as a form of useful feedback.[28] The article explains that psychologists have shown that optimism helps limit the impact of stress on the mind and body following difficult experiences. This is useful to note: adopting an optimistic approach gives people access to their own cognitive toolkit, enabling calmer analysis of what might have gone wrong and consideration of alternative options that could be more effective.

Pain and disappointment affect people in different ways, and dealing with these experiences isn't easy

---

28 'Resilience', *Psychology Today*, no date, www.psychologytoday.com/gb/basics/resilience, accessed 20 October 2020

for many of us. The psychologists explored what those who are more resilient do to carry on, emotionally and mentally, after the death of a loved one, a job loss, severe illness or another setback. Their learning may help others become more resilient.

Are you someone who believes that setbacks are the result of your own weaknesses, or are you able to identify contributing factors that are specific and temporary? Are you a perfectionist, or are you able to accept that life is a mix of difficulties and triumphs? In each of these examples, the latter trait is linked to greater levels of resilience.

Positive actions that reduce stress can also increase resilience, so it's important that you get enough sleep, eat healthily and exercise regularly. If you look after your body, you will be better placed to care for your mind. Cultivating close relationships can mean you are better able to find support when stressed. And living according to your values and morals has also been linked to higher resilience.

### POWER UP WITH DAME JULIE A KENNY DBE DL

'My first husband left me three months before I turned forty, and they say life begins at forty. I had such a rubbish upbringing and if you want to avoid going down the same route, you have to change your thought process. At forty, I decided that was the time to change. We were doing well at that time, employing 100 people, turning over millions and making a difference in the community, but still, I didn't love myself. I didn't think I was good enough so I read lots of books, I did counselling and hypnosis. I did some neuro-linguistic programming (NLP) and the NLP is what changed my life. I joined an academy group and found that I was actually advising others on how to tackle things. My confidence built and I wanted to learn more. I read self-help and business books.'

## Failure can be a good thing

To fail is deeply human; everyone, no matter what their background, skillset or life story, will fail spectacularly at least once in their life. Just because failure is commonplace, however, doesn't mean that experiencing a major loss or setback is easy or fun, or that it's widely accepted in a winner-takes-all culture that prioritises success at all costs. Learning to be OK with making mistakes, big or small, is a critical skill that is tied not only to resilience but also to future success. One recent study, for example, found that young scientists who experienced a significant setback early in their career actually went on to greater success than scientists who had seen early wins.[29]

One way of accepting that making mistakes is OK is to recognise that we cannot choose to avoid them if

29  S Allen, 'Early career failures can make you stronger in the long run', *Kellogg Insight*, 2019, https://insight.kellogg.northwestern.edu/article/early-setbacks-failure-career-success, accessed 20 October 2020

we want to live a fulfilling life. After talking about her own experiences of failure in a speech that she gave to the alumni of Harvard University, JK Rowling said, 'It is impossible to live without failing at something, unless you live so cautiously that you might as well not have lived at all – in which case, you fail by default.'[30]

### POWER UP WITH LINDA PLANT

'If you fall down and fail, don't worry. Don't be afraid to ask for help; don't be afraid to fail, because failure will set you up for success next time.'

# Take opportunities

Less than six months after starting my business, we had secured an application-form screening contract with a global investment bank. Part of the job required one of us to be at their London office in Canary Wharf one day a week. I loved this assignment, as the energy in Canary Wharf is palpable. The suited people politely queuing behind the Perspex screen at the Tube station, and the buzzing shopping centre there, are among the most iconic sights in London.

---

30  JK Rowling, 'Harvard Commencement Address to the Annual Meeting of the Harvard Alumni Association', 5 June 2008, www. jkrowling.com/harvard-commencement-address, accessed 16 September 2020

One lunchtime, I was scrolling through LinkedIn as I sat eating a sandwich in one of the Pret shops in the Canary Wharf shopping centre. I noticed a post from James Caan, who I had connected with a couple of years previously. He was running a competition to find a 'recruitment entrepreneur'. I read the post with growing excitement. James was looking to find someone with an idea or in the early stages of trading who he could mentor and invest £500,000 in. Clearly, that was me! I rang my business partner: 'Simon, I've seen this post on LinkedIn… we have to enter!' Simon agreed it sounded interesting and said he was up for it if I put an entry together.

I pulled together our entry, carefully following the rules on content and word count. I then decided to tap up David, an old friend at one of the big recruitment agencies I had worked with while in my previous role. David is head of project management at the agency and is an excellent marketing man. I sent the submission to David and asked him to be critical, suggesting areas we could make punchier to ensure it was a strong entry. After David had worked his magic, I was delighted with it. When I hit the submit button, pinging our entry over to James, I knew it would go somewhere. Do you ever have that feeling of certainty, your gut instinct? Whatever it is, I get it sometimes and I don't think it has ever been misplaced.

Sure enough, only a week or so later, I received an email from James's PA. 'James would like to meet you.' Waaah! I was so blooming excited to get that email and relished telling my business partner when it arrived. We were given two weeks to answer the brief for the next stage: 'Why should James partner with you?' The response was to be presented to James at his Mayfair office. I decided we needed to stand out and that a visual would help. I bought a massive piece of white card and got an artist friend to draw a winding path on it. I stuck pictures of Simon and me at the start of the path and included some photos along the first bit of the path to represent our journey so far – our previous work history, the services we were offering and the clients we had already won. The path then forked off in two directions – one showing us partnered with James and the other not, both with successful outcomes.

The day of the pitch came around quickly. We had a nightmare getting down to London, but thankfully we had planned to go the day before because we were due to meet a client. The day we travelled coincided with one of the worst storms ever in the UK and we ended up stranded in Peterborough for the best part of a day. We made it though, and I have a strong recollection of going into a Browns pub before the meeting to calm our nerves and have a last-minute run through before heading to his office.

As we approached James's office building, my nerves increased. The office was in a beautiful town-house style building in Mayfair. It was impressive and as we entered, I thought about how nice it would be to spend more time there. We were greeted by the receptionist and taken down to a board room, which felt rather like *Dragons' Den*. What wasn't so amusing was that there were ten of us 'finalists' in there. I was expecting to present our ideas one to one, so it was a little unnerving to know we were pitching against the competition. I made the most of the situation by chatting to everyone there and made a good contact with a lady based in Dubai.

James entered the room with the confidence you would expect of a successful businessman and TV star. He was wearing an expensive-looking suit and had a strong presence. He sat down and told us we each had three minutes to introduce ourselves and pitch our business. Simon and I were about halfway round the table, so we had a little time to compose ourselves. I was thrown somewhat by having a lot less time than I had expected. Today, I would absolutely nail that pitch with everything I have learned since, but this was only month six of being in business. Still, we did our best and his summary when we finished was, 'I get it, you are graduate recruitment experts who clearly know your stuff. Good.' He seemed to like our visual aid. As no one else had brought anything, it certainly made us stand out.

As we walked through Mayfair with that massive board (which I still have in our Newcastle office!) we reflected on the experience. It had been really exciting and I had enjoyed the thrill of meeting James and pitching our business. I was also concerned that if we won, we would be expected to relocate to London or at least spend a lot more time there, something I had wanted to avoid given that a key driver for setting up the business had been to have more time at home. My gut told me we wouldn't win the investment and, as usual, it was right. We received a polite email a day later: 'Thanks for coming in yesterday. It was really good to meet you both and we were certainly impressed by both your drive and ambition. And your presentation board!'

I don't regret having a go and on reflection, it was the right outcome for us. We dined out on the experience for months, if not years, afterwards. People in recruitment are always interested in hearing about the time we pitched to James Caan.

**POWER UP WITH LINDA PLANT**
'I never say no when I can say yes. Everyone gets opportunities; you've got to seize those opportunities. I don't believe in luck and I don't call it risk; I call it opportunity. In the early years, I had nothing to lose

because I had nothing. I considered the risk factor, but I seize opportunities. Everyone gets them, but can you seize them and what can you make of them?'

**POWER UP WITH DAME JULIE A KENNY DBE DL**
'If you are given an opportunity, grab it with both hands because you don't know where it's going to take you. You live a long time and you might grab the wrong opportunity, but something else will come and you'll learn such a lot from that.'

---

**TAKE ACTION**

Say yes to everything (within reason – trust your gut instinct) until you become so successful that you have to learn how to select more wisely and how to say no.

---

# Imposter syndrome

Imposter syndrome is a mixture of anxiety and a persistent inability to recognise one's own success. According to an article in the *Telegraph,* it can be crippling, destroying the careers and lives of its most chronic sufferers.[31] The syndrome was identified in 1978 by psychologists Pauline Clance and Suzanne

---

31   R Burn-Callander, 'Imposter syndrome: Women's silent career killer', *The Telegraph,* 2019, www.telegraph.co.uk/business/women-entrepreneurs/imposter-syndrome-women-careers, accessed 20 October 2020

Imes.[32] They believed that it only affected women, but subsequent research has shown that men are also affected. However, women tend to be more susceptible because they produce less testosterone – the confidence hormone.

I often hear my friends talking about imposter syndrome and it's clearly a real thing for many of my peers. My own imposter syndrome kicks in when I get asked to do something that feels a little out of my comfort zone. A key example of that would be the TEDx Talk I mentioned earlier. I know that many people apply for the opportunity to deliver a TEDx Talk. It was always in the back of my mind as a challenge I should put myself forward for in the future. When I was given the opportunity to do one off the back of my last book, I couldn't believe it.

When I had that first meeting with Lesley, as I described in the introduction to this book, I genuinely felt ill. I couldn't believe that my talk had gone from a work-related topic that I knew loads about and felt more comfortable speaking about to something far more personal. Why would anyone care about my backstory? I thought people would think me full of myself if I stood on that stage talking about my business success. I have never been so nervous as I was

32  P Clance and S Imes, 'The imposter phenomenon in high achieving women: Dynamics and therapeutic intervention', *Psychotherapy: Theory, Research and Practice*, 15 (3), 241–247

in the run-up to that talk. It seems silly now, but those nerves and huge waves of self-doubt were all-encompassing for weeks before I got on that stage.

As with many things, the anxiety I felt in the run-up completely dissipated the moment I left the stage. It resurfaced momentarily when the TEDx Talk was released on YouTube. Should I share the link? What will people think? Sod it, I thought. The effort and emotion that had gone into that talk meant that I had to share it, and it has only generated positive responses so I needn't have been so worried.

Here's how to battle imposter syndrome:

- **Accept it.** As you can see from the stories I've shared, imposter syndrome still rears its head despite proven success. It can be managed with time and support, but it is unlikely to go away.

- **Share your feelings.** Talk to your support group – the people who think you're awesome and will lift you up when any self-doubt creeps in.

- **Be rational.** Write down all of your achievements – you will have way more than you think, so ask friends to contribute to your list. Accept that these achievements are yours and built on facts.

Remember that imposter syndrome tends to affect high achievers who set far higher standards for themselves than other people. If you look at it that way, it's more of a positive thing, right?

## POWER UP WITH KATY LEESON

'Famous people such as Meryl Streep and Albert Einstein had imposter syndrome! Embrace your imposter. It means you are pushing yourself, so you are in growth mode. Ignore it and try it. I took a lot of time to sit back and learn my values. I had never done that before but in doing that, I've learned that learning is one of my values, so if I don't have a little imposter syndrome then I'm not embracing my values.'

## POWER UP WITH JACQUELINE DE ROJAS CBE

'I interviewed a lot of people as part of London Tech Week. Last week I interviewed Tony Blair. Whether you agree with his politics or not is irrelevant. He is incredibly learned, an ex-barrister, has won three consecutive elections as a Labour leader, is incredibly articulate. So, do you think I had imposter syndrome? I had papers stuck to every surface with all the questions on my screen! Was I over-prepared? For sure. Did I have imposter syndrome? Completely. I literally felt it in my fingers. To overcome that, I take steps to control it by being prepared – probably over-prepared.'

---

## TAKE ACTION

Create a folder in your email inbox, give it a name – mine's called 'nice things' – and file any nice comments or feedback from your clients, colleagues and contacts. Every so often, when you doubt yourself, pop into the folder and read some of the messages. It will give you a real boost and help you to beat imposter syndrome.

---

## Social media

I've no doubt that you are familiar with social media. You're likely to be on several platforms and have a preference for one or two over the others. Social media connects millions of people all over the world, and it's a great way to keep in touch with friends and share and document exciting memories. However, what you say and do on social media also determines how others, including potential employers and clients, perceive you and your values. As Amy Jo Martin, CEO of Digital Royalty tweeted, 'Every time you post a photo or update your status, you are contributing to your own digital footprint and personal brand.'[33] Some employers will look up candidates on social media before making them a job offer and some will monitor content posted by people in the job, so it's important to represent yourself well professionally on all social media platforms.

I've outlined the key dos and don'ts to help you get started:

---

33   AJ Martin (@AmyJoMartin), 'Every time you post a photo...' [tweet], 13 June 2018, https://twitter.com/amyjomartin/status/10069876611 38067456?lang=en-gb, accessed 16 September 2020

## The dos

- **Do search for yourself on the internet.** You'll be amazed by how much information is captured online. Make sure there's nothing on the first or second page of the search results that could show you in a bad light. If there is, get it removed. Make sure you check for images that might appear from old sites you no longer use.

- **Do cleanse your social media profiles.** Getting rid of any social media content that doesn't show you in the best light is the easiest way to make sure recruiters and employers don't see it. I'm not saying you need to delete all your precious memories – just remove those that are less forgiving, or at least change your privacy settings.

- **Do check your privacy settings.** If your Facebook, Twitter and Instagram accounts aren't suitable for public viewing, make sure they're private.

- **Do be careful what you post.** You never know who might view your profiles, so don't post anything inappropriate.

## The don'ts

- **Don't hide.** Employers and recruiters will want to see that you have a social media presence, so don't go completely off-grid.

- **Don't post anything you wouldn't want your grandparents to see.** Keep it clean. Remember, information remains on the internet for a long time.

- **Don't connect to everybody.** Think twice before accepting requests from friends on your LinkedIn account. Your connections should be relevant to your industry.

- **Don't overshare.** Don't post anything that you'll regret later or that could damage your chances of securing the job of your dreams. Be mindful of what you share and how you share it.

If you're searching for a job, LinkedIn is a useful platform to be active on. Make sure that your profile is up to date and that you have completed every section. Follow companies you would like to work for, join relevant groups and interact with posts. When you meet people at events, send them a LinkedIn invitation to connect within one day. They are more likely to accept when they remember who you are, and once you have connected you can continue your conversations and start building relationships.

LinkedIn has so much value for those wanting to progress their careers and or run their own business. When I was in the corporate world, I was often approached by headhunters. As an entrepreneur, certain posts can attract business and I've won significant deals off the back of specific LinkedIn posts that have been spotted by my target audience. Most people don't post enough, so they miss out on the opportunities this can bring. The thing with regular posting is that it takes time, but it becomes quicker as you get to know your audience, and you can be clever about preparing your content. I often prepare my posts during 'dead time', such as commuting or travelling, simply drafting posts in the notes section of my phone, ready to share at appropriate times. You can learn about how often to post and when, specifically for each platform, by doing a bit of research. Gary Vaynerchuk is well known in this area and has some great books and YouTube content if you'd like to explore this topic further.[34]

**POWER UP WITH KATY LEESON**

'I use LinkedIn, Twitter and Instagram for work but use each platform differently. Find your why, what your differences are and why people would want to follow you. It's about the consistency as well, but to get that, you have to find something you're passionate about. I found writing articles was getting a good response but I found it a chore so the consistency wasn't there, so find a topic you're interested in and something people find useful, because that's how you get your following and you will want to be consistent.'

---

34  See his YouTube channel at www.youtube.com/user/ GaryVaynerchuk.

## POWER UP WITH ALICE HALL

'For business to consumer (B2C), Instagram and TikTok are great. TikTok presents massive opportunities right now, as it's not massively monetised so it presents organic growth opportunities. I always advise people to jump on the latest platform and the latest features. Instagram is very much a platform that you can build a brand and convert on, but it's tough now. It takes a lot of content production. Instagram stories are great, as they are a little more laid back, but a lot of people are intimidated by the feed element. For business to business (B2B) and personal profile building in business, LinkedIn is brilliant. The great thing about LinkedIn is not a lot of people produce content. There's a lot of people checking and lurking but if you produce content, you're more likely to be featured in the feed. Investing a bit of time can have massive rewards!'

---

## TAKE ACTION

There are social media superstars for every platform, so find the platform that is most relevant to you and your industry and seek out those who excel. Work out what you like about their content and let that shape your own style. Research optimum posting times and frequencies for your platform choice and commit to trying it out for a month. That should be long enough for you to see the benefits and continue.

---

## Personal brand and values

In the pre-internet days, your personal brand was pretty much just your business card. Unless you were high profile in the media or somebody who featured strongly as the face of advertising, few people would have heard of you. In today's highly public world, where every little action is discussed at length on social media, you are far less anonymous.

Your personal brand is how you promote yourself. It is the unique combination of skills, experience and personality that you want the world to see linked to you. It is the telling of your story, and how this reflects your conduct, behaviour, spoken and unspoken words, and attitudes.

The easiest and most effective way to have a strong personal brand is via social media. As I said earlier, it's best to stick to one or two platforms, as if you spread yourself too thinly, it can be hard to keep up with them all – trust me, I've tried! I made the choice to focus mostly on LinkedIn and Twitter as that is where my audience spends most of their time. I try to post on Twitter a few times a day and on LinkedIn a few times a week.

A few things happened that made me realise I had nailed these two platforms. Firstly, my connections and

followers started growing quickly; but more importantly, so did the engagement on my posts. A good
LinkedIn post these days on my profile will get 30,000
to 50,000 views which is certainly above average. The
other thing I noticed was that when I was out and about
meeting clients, they often referred to something I had
posted about – eg 'Well done on winning that award
last week – I saw it on LinkedIn.' I have a couple of
funny stories that highlighted the progress I had made
on these platforms. The first was on LinkedIn when a
guy I vaguely knew asked me to promote a product he
was selling and called me a recruitment influencer. The
second is even more hilarious.

A couple of years ago I was walking down Pink Lane
in Newcastle on the way to a meeting at Pink Lane
Coffee. As I was walking downhill towards the coffee
shop, I spotted this tiny blonde lady outside chatting
on the phone and waving at me frantically. My eyesight
is pretty good so even from a distance I knew I did not
know this lady. As I walked closer, she became more
animated and I had to make a quick decision – did I
pretend I knew her or come clean? I decided to come
clean. 'I'm so sorry, but I have absolutely no idea who
you are,' I said in my best friendly voice. The lady,
Kate, replied, 'Oh my God, I'm so embarrassed. I follow you on Twitter and just feel like I totally know
you.' We had a good laugh, which broke the ice, and
I asked her about what she did. Both of us were there

for separate meetings in the same coffee shop, but we swapped cards and arranged to meet for a coffee another time.

On meeting up a few weeks later, I learned that Kate delivered the training for coaching qualifications (among other things). I ended up completing my Level 7 coaching and mentoring qualification with her, when I got to know her better. We've since been on two mastermind groups together and have become friends.

## Why would you want a personal brand?

Your personal brand can be vital to you professionally. It is how you present yourself to your current and potential employers and to your clients. It gives you the opportunity to ensure that people see you in the way you want them to. Your personal brand is what makes you memorable – for good or bad reasons! It is your personal brand that helps you stand out from the thousands of other people like you.

Creating a personal brand requires extensive self-reflection, which is a useful skill to develop anyway. It helps if you know yourself – which surprisingly few people do. Most people find it extremely difficult to describe themselves, although they often find it easier to explain how they want to be. This is where values come into play.

## Values

Values help you establish a sense of purpose and direction for your personal brand. They act as guideposts that assist you in evaluating choices in your life. Values drive you and help you commit to your life. Often, the reason people are unhappy at work is because their values no longer align with what they are doing. When you're crafting a personal brand, you must understand your core values because they are the heart of who you are.

**POWER UP WITH JACQUELINE DE ROJAS CBE**
'I choose not to work in a culture that I am uncomfortable with. I choose to spend my time in a culture that will embrace me and that I can be inspired by versus a culture that does not serve me. For anybody choosing a new career, I would check out the culture first. Culture trumps strategy and you will thrive in a culture that is aligned with your values. I also heard a brilliant quote recently by John Amaechi, which said, "Culture can be defined by the worst behaviour tolerated" – so true.'

You need to consider what's important to *you*, as we all have different values and motivations. Ask yourself these three simple questions:

- What is important to me?

- What are my values?

- What motivates me?

The answers to these questions will help you work out what you need to be happy and motivated in your career and how you want your personal brand to portray you.

Employers are putting more emphasis on values, but it can be difficult to work out what your values actually are. It might feel much easier to list skills and then try to manipulate these into values, but skills and values are different things. Values are lasting beliefs or ideals about what's good or bad and what's desirable or undesirable. They have a major influence on your behaviour and attitude. You can find a list of organisational values by doing a little digging on an employer's website. If you can't find them, you could always get in touch with them to ask if they have a document they're willing to share with you.

Before looking at an organisation's values, it's important to establish your own – then you can make a comparison. Use the following list of values to start thinking about what is important to you. Write your top ten values on ten separate pieces of paper. Then, one by one, throw away one piece of paper with a value that is less of a priority to you than the others.

Stop when you only have three or four left. You might be attracted to many of the words on this list but if you value everything, you value nothing: you need to be able to distinguish between them and prioritise. Do this activity with a friend or two if you fancy it, as the discussion you could have afterwards would be really interesting and help you understand your responses and those of your friends in more depth.

| Abundance | Consciousness | Fairness | Knowledge | Resilience |
|---|---|---|---|---|
| Acceptance | Consistency | Faith | Leadership | Resourcefulness |
| Accomplishment | Contentment | Fame | Learning | Respect |
| Accuracy | Contribution | Family | Liberty | Restraint |
| Achievement | Control | Fearlessness | Logic | Sacrifice |
| Acknowledgement | Coolness | Fidelity | Love | Satisfaction |
| Activeness | Co-operation | Financial independence | Loyalty | Security |
| Adaptability | Correctness | Fitness | Making a difference | Self-control |
| Adventure | Courage | Flexibility | Mastery | Selflessness |
| Affection | Creativity | Focus | Mindfulness | Self-reliance |
| Affluence | Credibility | Freedom | Motivation | Serenity |
| Agility | Curiosity | Friendliness | Neatness | Service |
| Altruism | Daring | Frugality | Obedience | Significance |
| Ambition | Decisiveness | Fun | Open-mindedness | Silence |
| Appreciation | Dependability | Generosity | Optimism | Simplicity |
| Assertiveness | Determination | Giving | Organisation | Sincerity |
| Attractiveness | Devotion | Grace | Originality | Skilfulness |
| Availability | Dignity | Gratitude | Passion | Solitude |
| Awareness | Diligence | Growth | Peace | Spirituality |

*Continued*

| | | | | |
|---|---|---|---|---|
| Balance | Diplomacy | Happiness | Perfection | Spontaneity |
| Beauty | Discipline | Harmony | Perseverance | Stability |
| Being the best | Discovery | Health | Philanthropy | Strength |
| Belonging | Diversity | Helpfulness | Playfulness | Success |
| Boldness | Drive | Heroism | Pleasantness | Support |
| Bravery | Duty | Honesty | Pleasure | Sympathy |
| Brilliance | Education | Humility | Popularity | Synergy |
| Calmness | Effectiveness | Humour | Power | Teamwork |
| Challenge | Efficiency | Hygiene | Practicality | Traditionalism |
| Charity | Elegance | Imagination | Pragmatism | Timeliness |
| Charm | Empathy | Independence | Precision | Tranquillity |
| Clarity | Endurance | Insightfulness | Preparedness | Trustworthiness |
| Cleanliness | Energy | Inspiration | Privacy | Truth |
| Comfort | Enjoyment | Integrity | Professionalism | Understanding |
| Commitment | Enthusiasm | Intelligence | Prosperity | Uniqueness |
| Compassion | Excellence | Intimacy | Realism | Variety |
| Completion | Excitement | Introversion | Reason | Victory |
| Composure | Experience | Intuition | Recognition | Virtue |
| Concentration | Expertise | Joy | Recreation | Vision |
| Congruency | Expressiveness | Justice | Relaxation | Warmth |
| Connection | Extroversion | Kindness | Reliability | Wisdom |

Now you have identified what is important to you, you have a frame of reference to refer to when interacting with others and when posting online.

### POWER UP WITH AYESHA NAYYAR
'People expect lawyers to be dry. There is an impression that professionals are dry and boring, but we are colourful and individual people. You can bring

your personality to the table. You've got to have a USP. I'm a lawyer but I am an individual.

'What you see is what I am. It's important to put your true image out there. You've got to conduct yourself a certain way. Everything I do now in my professional and personal life, I take my responsibility very seriously.'

---

**TAKE ACTION**

You are who Google says you are. Have you ever googled your name? Do it now, ideally changing your settings so your device doesn't remember your browsing history. You may find that other people share your name, but when you do see search results that mention you, do they show what you want the world to see? Ideally, you want to see your name in items listed on the first page. If nothing comes up, you have work to do. That can be as simple as posting regularly on open social media profiles.

---

# Growth mindset

I came across the growth versus fixed mindset theory a few years ago and it totally resonated. Many people believe that Professor Carol Dweck's theory of the growth mindset has created a new formula for success.[35] A growth mindset is all about persevering

---

35  C Dweck, *Mindset: Changing the way you think to fulfil your potential* (Robinson, 2017)

when the going gets tough and turning failure into useable information. Developing a growth mindset will teach you to embrace failure and find new ways of succeeding.

Dweck found in her research that one of the most basic beliefs we carry about ourselves has to do with how we view what we consider to be our personality. A fixed mindset assumes that our character, intelligence and creative ability are static givens, which we can't change. Success is the affirmation of that inherent intelligence: an assessment of how those givens measure up against an equally fixed standard. Striving for success and avoiding failure at all costs becomes a way of maintaining our sense of being smart or skilled. A growth mindset, on the other hand, thrives on challenge and sees failure not as evidence of unintelligence but as an opportunity for growth and for stretching our existing abilities. Out of these two mindsets, which we manifest from an early age, springs a great deal of our behaviour, our relationship with success and failure in professional and personal contexts, and ultimately our capacity for happiness.

What makes the growth mindset so appealing, Dweck found, is that it creates a passion for learning rather than a hunger for approval. Its hallmark is the conviction that human qualities (such as intelligence and creativity) and even relational capacities (like love and friendship) can be cultivated through effort and intentional practice. Not only are people with this mindset not disheartened by failure, but they don't actually see themselves as failing in those situations; they see themselves as learning.

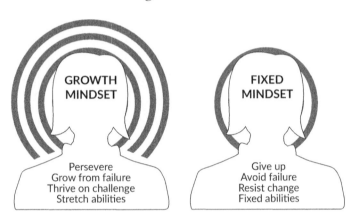

GROWTH MINDSET
Persevere
Grow from failure
Thrive on challenge
Stretch abilities

FIXED MINDSET
Give up
Avoid failure
Resist change
Fixed abilities

Really, this concept isn't anything new. We've all come across the fluffy 'You can do it, girl!' videos, memes and self-help books. What makes Dweck's research different is her thorough investigations into how the mind, especially the developing mind, works, identifying not only the core drivers of those mindsets but also how they can be reprogrammed. Dweck and her team found that people with the fixed mindset see risk and effort as potential giveaways of their inadequacies, revealing that they come up short in some way, but the relationship between mindset and effort is a two-way street.

Carol Dweck's growth mindset emphasises how intelligence alone isn't enough. It's what we do with it that's important. It's so easy to throw in the towel when things get tricky, but don't give up. Growth mindset is all about recognising that those bumps in the road are part of the learning process. It's normal, and it's the terrain that leads to success.

Think of failure as data. It's information that you can use next time to develop and grow. Yes, I know failure hurts (for everyone) and that sinking feeling is universal. Grab your growth mindset and get back in the saddle, as the growth mindset is all about effort. It's the hallmark of a fixed mindset to expect things to be easy. Success demands working hard, learning from failure and refining your performance as you progress your career.

**POWER UP WITH LARA MORGAN**

'Layer on the humility, be the learner, never be arrogant. I'm still faking it; I end up brain-picking some brilliant people. I called an awesome entrepreneur who scared me shitless the other day but by having the desire to learn, it pays me dividends and gets me shortcuts and accelerates our opportunities. You have to put energy into the learning. You can't stand still in business. Business will eat you alive.

'I'm an idiot. It took me a long time to realise investing in myself wasn't a ridiculous expense. It took me probably nine years to invest in my own strategic intelligence and my business nous and then I went on a course at Cranfield called Business Growth Development.'

## POWER UP WITH ALICE HALL

'If I'm driving to work in the morning, I have half an hour to learn something new. I listen to podcasts. I like the Boss Babe podcasts. They talk about the highs and lows and self-care, loads of topics. I like Tom Bilyeu; he talks about innovative things. There is something called the Blog Millionaire; I like that. There are a raft of influencers producing content and I like hearing about their journeys along the way.'

## TAKE ACTION

Try this short activity:

Think about all the skills you have built throughout your life and how you have advanced them. No matter what your mindset is, surely you can think of something that you were not good at doing when you started it but you eventually got the hang of.

For example, think about your first day in a new job. Did you show up having the routine and productivity that you have today, or did you have to go through some trial and error to learn how to be good at what you do? You probably had to 'practise' your job each day by facing various problems that you had to work to solve.

Think about what this process was like – whether it's your current job or something more basic, such as driving a car. Reflecting and recognising the skills you have already improved will help you be more open to the idea that you *can* learn and improve. Once you *do* start to learn a new skill, reflect on your progress and what you have learned up to this point and keep a record of how that progress continues to change.

---

# 5
# Final Thoughts

## Pivot (if you're not happy, change things)

Remember my story about the manager who told me my work was shit? That was probably the first example of me not being happy with something and working out I needed to do something to change things. Things rarely change without intervention, so if you aren't happy, make a decision and then take action to change your life. The same advice applies in careers and in business. You might have studied for a particular career only to discover that you actually hate it. You might worry about what people will think if you change direction or fear that you aren't qualified for anything else. That's not true! You will always have transferable skills that will add value to a new career – or business idea, if you are an entrepreneur. There is strength in identifying when something isn't working and taking action to improve the situation. Find work that you love, and it will never feel like work. That is career success summed up.

This advice links to failing fast. If your chosen direction isn't working out then acknowledge that, consider your options and take action quickly. If you're in a job you hate, is it the job or is it the organisation? Talk it through with a trusted friend or mentor to work out the issues. If it's the organisation, seek out alternatives that more closely meet your values and get applying. If it's the job itself, spend time working out what it is you enjoy doing and work out how to move into another role, either in your current organisation or by applying elsewhere. If you are an entrepreneur and your current idea doesn't work, be honest with yourself, seek advice and try something else. Whatever your current predicament, you will have learned more than you realise and you can take this learning elsewhere.

Try these top tips for a successful pivot:

1. Identify the current situation

2. Seek advice

3. Consider your options

4. Take action

5. Review – going back to the start of this list if you need to

**POWER UP WITH SHERRY COUTU CBE**

'Every single individual between graduation and retirement has on average twenty-five different jobs, with six or seven identifiable career themes, so you shouldn't be totally stressed about your first job. If you think about your first job, you probably have had work experience or internships before that and that will make you more capable of making a wise decision for your first permanent role. We need skills of agility, problem-solving, communication, so we can navigate ourselves through unclear waters. It's more exciting when you look at it as a journey.'

## Advice we would like to pass on

I'm sure the stories and advice from the women I interviewed as part of my research for this book will have resonated with many of you. I asked them each to give the advice they wish they had known as they started their careers, and this is what they shared.

'Get your head around finances. If you don't know the difference between profit and loss and, most importantly, if you're not costing correctly, then you will fail. It doesn't mat-

ter how clever you are, how engaging, what a great salesperson; if you don't know your numbers and where your cash is, you're toast.'
— Lara Morgan

'I don't have imposter syndrome now but certainly I did when I was in my twenties. How I used to cope was I used to power-dress. I sat on the board of directors for the global trade association for the craft and hobby industry, and I was the youngest person and one of only a handful of women. It was all older men in suits, so I would power-dress in a suit and act and behave how I felt that room needed me to act and behave. I was on the board for six years and by the end of it, I stopped trying to be someone else and just tried to be me.

'It was the same with *Dragons' Den* when I did my first interview. The feedback I got from the producers was, "It was a great interview, but you were just a little bit too nice compared with what we normally have on the show." I took the decision that I could pretend to be somebody I'm not but I learned that just doesn't work so I'm just going to be me; if I'm not, it's not going to be right. Since I made that shift, I don't suffer from imposter syndrome any more, because I have self-belief that I am good enough to be wherever I want to be – the line-up in the Den or sitting around the board table. I earned the right to be there.'

— Sara Davies MBE

'Work hard. There is no substitute for hard work in your career. Surround yourself with other like-minded, hardworking, ambitious people because you are very much influenced by the company that you keep. If you can become a group of hardworking individuals, your network will inspire you. Use all the tools available to build up your network.'

— Ayesha Nayyar

'Don't be afraid to fail. It's hard to get your head into that but I have made the biggest movements forward when I've made a mistake. Everyone makes errors and mistakes, but it is how you learn from those and make sure you don't do them again. That's been my biggest career learning. At school, you are taught to pass things and you're ingrained with the fear of failing. But failing is where I've had the biggest learnings. We say "lessons, not losses" at work when we don't win a pitch.'

— Katy Leeson

'If you find yourself doing something that you don't love, then you should stop. That is really clear. If your current skillset prevents

149

you from moving on, then in your spare time, upskill yourself. There are a huge number of things out there for free, such as YouTube and Coursera. It is really important that people love their work and if you don't like it, it's not good for you. Someone will love the job you have so move on to something you love which opens the space for someone else. Maintain that balance and thinking about what we are here for. Chase your dreams and do what you love. Solve problems that are important. Believe in yourself.'
— Sherry Coutu CBE

'Realistic goals are important. Have big dreams but walk before you can run. Be honest with yourself. If you're motivated and driven, with the capacity to grow, that will see you through. Those are the things that have carried me through and will carry everyone through whatever. Value relationships.'
— Linda Plant

'My self-limiting belief was that you had to be a man to make it. In order to fit in, I took on male characteristics of language and discipline. I even wore a tie to work at times. There was an edge I had which I have since substituted for soft power. I have come to realise that the soft power is so important. Tolerance, kindness and compassion are stronger opportunities for us to grow and enable others to thrive in our teams.'

— Jacqueline de Rojas CBE

'One: aim high and then deliver. Two: failure is learning. Three: read. Take a look at business headlines so whoever you are at the table with, you know what is happening in the business and in the world.'

— Stephanie Kauffman

'You have to believe in yourself. You have to believe you can achieve something. I've had lots of people ask me how I've done it over the years: is it nature, is it nurture? And actually, you have to have focus, determination, a can-do attitude, positivity. I was asked in 1988 where I wanted to be at an exhibition. I said, "You see that stand over there, that's where I want to be," and that stand was the largest supplier (in our industry) at that time. We'd only been going two years at that time and the man who asked the question laughed at me. Four years later, I wrote to him when we were number one. It was such an outrageous aspiration, but no aspiration is outrageous

if you believe in it and if it is your focus and determination.'
— Dame Julie A Kenny DBE DL

'I read that if you build your personal brand then you will be able to sell whatever ventures you then go into. If you focus purely on the brand you work for, you can't take that with you. Time spent building your own brand means you can then do so much with it.'
— Alice Hall

'If people are disparaging or belittling towards you, don't be downhearted, see that as a spur – know that you are better than they think, and do better!'
— Margaret Casely-Hayford CBE

The advice I would like to leave you with is to continue to learn forever, as it keeps the passion for your career alive and your mind young. I would advise learning about your finances early on in that learning. As children, we are encouraged to save, get good jobs and buy a nice house. There is some sense in that, of course, but I often see friends who have mortgage payments, expensive (and unnecessary) car payments and all the material trappings that outwardly demonstrate success. Living this way is expensive and can bring a lot of stress and unhappiness.

# Pay it forward

With hard work and determination, you will be successful at whatever you prioritise. Once you get to a point where you have learned things that can be shared, my wish is that you start to look for opportunities to pay it forward. Can you mentor the new girl at work? If you have started a business, can you spot someone at a networking event who is in the early days of her own start-up and take her for a coffee? Can you speak at a school or an event to encourage and motivate the next generation? The answer to all of these questions is, of course, yes – so go out there and be brilliant.

**POWER UP WITH DAME JULIE A KENNY DBE DL**
'Every hour I've donated to volunteering in free time, I've had that back in learning. I've been able to bring that learning back to improve myself and my business. What goes around comes around. If you're interested in helping others, it is a fantastic experience. In 2002, I was honoured by the Queen with a CBE for services within the region.'

**POWER UP WITH MARGARET CASELY-HAYFORD CBE**
'Because there's so much inequality of opportunity, I personally try to offer mentoring, guidance, help with CVs, introductions, talks about my own personal experience and journey, sponsorship and investment. In my view, until there's greater fairness, the whole support package will remain necessary; and I try to

encourage those who make decisions that impact on the recruitment, appointment and promotion of others in corporate environments to do better!'

## Be bold and take action!

Finally, be bold and take action. Some of the women who contributed to this book are business heroes of mine. I've watched Sara on stage delivering an inspirational speech at a business event (pre-*Dragons' Den* – she's in a whole new league now!) and admired Linda grilling candidates on *The Apprentice*. I spotted opportunities to connect with them and the other women I interviewed, and I invited them to be involved. Without taking action, I wouldn't have had the privilege of sharing their stories and advice with you.

# Acknowledgements

I would like to thank everyone who has encouraged me and helped me to get this book published. At Rethink Press, the team have been terrific as always, offering constant support and encouragement.

I want to thank my team at SRS who have given up their own time to read, give feedback and format this book.

Thank you to Simone Roche MBE for writing the foreword, for her unwavering faith and for introductions to some incredible women.

My KPI 26 accountability group also deserve a shout out as they kept me on the right track for months, holding me to account on a weekly basis so that I made the progress required to meet the publishing deadlines.

## Contributors

One of the most fun things about writing this book was the opportunity it gave me to speak to so many inspirational women. I feel like I learned so much from our conversations and thank each and every one of you for sharing your time and experiences with honesty and candour.

### Margaret Casely-Hayford CBE

 Margaret Casely-Hayford has been a non-executive member of the board of the Co-op Group since 2016. She was appointed Chair of Shakespeare's Globe in January 2018, the same year in which she was appointed Chancellor of Coventry University.

She was Director of Legal Services and Company Secretary for the John Lewis Partnership for nine years. Before that she worked for twenty years with City law firm Dentons, where she had been a partner and jointly led an award-winning team in planning and development work. She has now retired from executive roles.

Her portfolio includes advising young entrepreneurs; supporting and advising organisations on governance; and advising those, in particular, women and BAME or LGTBQ+ people, who wish to embark upon board careers. She is passionate about establishing diversity on boards and is an ambassador for Board Apprentice.

She champions better governance and democratic processes. In 2020 she was appointed to the Institute of Directors' Governance Advisory Board and made a fellow of the Centre for Public Impact.

Her passion for education also sees her acting as Chair of the Advisory Board for the award-winning Ultra Education, an enterprise that teaches entrepreneurial skills to primary school children, and as patron of the John Staples Society, a body created across the Leathersellers' Federation of Schools, to develop social mobility by providing opportunities and access.

Margaret is a trustee of the Radcliffe Trust, which supports the development of skills in classical music and traditional arts and crafts.

She chaired a diversity review of the Carnegie and Kate Greenaway Awards for CILIP (the Libraries

Association); served on a panel that oversaw the 2018 strategic review of the British Council, making recommendations to the Foreign Secretary; and has recently been asked by Oriel College, Oxford, to participate in the commission established to consider whether Cecil Rhodes' statue should stand or fall.

In 2018, upon ending her term as trustee and chair of international development charity ActionAid UK, she was awarded a CBE in the Queen's Honours list, for services to charity and for promoting diversity. She was also awarded an Honorary Fellowship of her former University college: Somerville, Oxford.

## Sherry Coutu CBE

Sherry Coutu is a serial entrepreneur and angel investor who serves on the boards of companies, charities and universities. She chairs or has chaired Founders4Schools, Workfinder, Raspberry Pi (Trading), Digital Boost and the Scaleup Institute. She also serves as a non-executive director of Pearson plc and London Stock Exchange plc, and as a trustee of Raspberry Pi Foundation.

With more than sixty angel investments, three initial public offerings (IPOs), and numerous joint ventures and acquisitions behind her, Sherry has extensive experience in early and mid-stage companies, having held senior positions in product management, research, finance and operations.

Philanthropically, she supports Founders4Schools, the Prince's Trust and the Crick Institute.

Sherry has an MBA from Harvard, an MSc (with distinction) from the London School of Economics and a BA (Hons with distinction) from the University of British Columbia, Canada. She has been awarded honorary PhDs from the University of Bristol, the University of Manchester and the Open University for her work in education and the economy.

She was appointed Commander of the Order of the British Empire (CBE) for services to entrepreneurship in the New Year's Honours List 2013.

## Sara Davies MBE

Sara Davies MBE is the founder and creative director of Crafter's Companion. She was born in Coundon to entrepreneurial parents, Frank and Susan, and today lives in County Durham with her husband Simon and her children, Oliver and Charlie.

Sara established Crafter's Companion while studying for a business management degree at the University of York. During a placement at a small craft company, she spotted a gap in the market for a tool that could create bespoke envelopes for handmade cards. With help from her retired engineer father, Sara designed and launched a ground-breaking craft product called The Enveloper.

After securing a slot on TV shopping channel Ideal World, The Enveloper became an instant hit, selling 1,500 units in the first 2 minutes and 30,000 units within 6 months of the initial demonstration. This demand led Sara to develop her first line of innovative products for the craft market. She left university with a first-class honours degree and a business turning over half a million pounds.

Today, Crafter's Companion is a household name in the industry. It has expanded its range of papercraft products to include sewing and needlecraft items, in addition to its own brand of art materials, Spectrum Noir.

The company designs, manufactures and sells its craft-related products to customers across 40 countries and employs more than 200 people worldwide.

It continues to celebrate its North East roots, with a head office, warehouse and store in County Durham, and has established stores in Chesterfield and Evesham. Crafter's Companion also has a US head office and warehouse in Corona, California.

Crafter's Companion has appeared in the *Sunday Times*' SME Export Track 100 list four times. It ranked at number 73 in 2019, 31 in 2018 (after experiencing 72% year-on-year-growth in export sales), 52 in 2017 and number 26 in 2015.

To date, the business has proudly collected more than thirty awards for the company's achievements and for Sara's accomplishments as an entrepreneur, in addition to a multitude of craft industry awards for its innovative products. These include the Ernst & Young UK Emerging Entrepreneur, Shell Livewire Young Entrepreneur, Women of the Future Award and the Stevie Women in Business Award for Young Entrepreneur, as well as International Business of the Year at the Federation of Small Businesses Awards.

Sara has been recognised in the 'Who's Who of Britain's Business Elite' and CNBC's 'UK's Top Ten Brilliant Entrepreneurs', and she received the Creative Entrepreneur of the Year award at the Great British Entrepreneur Awards.

In 2016, Sara was presented with an MBE in Her Majesty's Birthday Honours List, for services to the economy.

Sara regularly features on the Create and Craft TV channel in the UK, in addition to the Home Shopping Network (HSN) in the US and QVC Germany. She was the founding chair of the board of directors at the Craft Hobby Association UK, now known as the AFCI-UK, which complements her role on the board of the affiliate US chapter.

Most recently, Sara was named as the youngest entrepreneur to join BBC Two's *Dragons' Den*. She is passionate about championing women in business, mentoring and the North East of England.

## Alice Hall

 Alice Hall is an entrepreneur from Newcastle upon Tyne. Starting her first business with £90 and growing it to £25 million turnover, she has gone on to set up various eCommerce businesses in the food, property and interior design sectors. Alice has been featured in Forbes 30 Under 30 and won a range of other prestigious awards.

## Stephanie Kauffman

Stephanie Kauffman is a managing partner of Tahoe Ventures, a strategic consulting and advisory firm. Stephanie advises on several areas for the firm, including growth acceleration, digital transformation, strategic alliances and post-mergers and acquisitions (M&A) marketing integration strategies for global brands, corporate investors, startups and non-profits.

A long-time marketing, strategy and brand partnerships leader at Universal Studios, Stephanie worked in various roles of increasing responsibility, eventually becoming the Senior Vice President, Global Brand Alliances, for the Studios' worldwide film, home entertainment and theme park businesses. Under her leadership, Universal forged landmark partnerships with global brands on blockbuster film and theme park integration, and marketing campaigns, including the multi-year *Fast & Furious* and Dodge franchise partnership. Stephanie was also a part of the leadership team that launched and built the global *Despicable Me/ Minions* consumer products and brand alliance franchise into a multibillion-dollar programme around the world. She has also held chief partnership roles with TripAdvisor and the Breast Cancer Research Foundation.

Stephanie serves on the board of directors for the International Women's Media Foundation, which champions and strengthens women's roles and voices in global media. She resides in the New York City suburbs with her husband and three stepchildren.

## Dame Julie A Kenny DBE DL

Dame Julie A Kenny is a successful entrepreneur based in South Yorkshire. Following the sale in 2016 of the award-winning Pyronix Limited, which she built from a startup in 1986, Julie continues her involvement in serving business and local communities. She currently holds several trustee/patron positions for diverse charitable organisations.

Julie is a chair and non-executive director of Robson Handling Technology Limited. She chairs Maltby Learning Trust, a multi-academy trust and sponsor which is governed by a board of directors; Sheffield Culture Collective; and the Wentworth Woodhouse Preservation Trust, which is committed to securing a sustainable future for the country house Wentworth Woodhouse, in Wentworth, near Rotherham. Julie is also a trustee of the National Coal Mining Museum of England and a director of Sheffield Theatres.

Having served as Intervention Commissioner with Rotherham Metropolitan Borough Council between 2015 and 2018, Julie's involvement in the promotion of her home town continues as a Rotherham Pioneer and an Ambition Rotherham Board Member.

Julie was honoured in Her Majesty the Queen's Birthday Honours List in June 2019 with a Damehood for her work with heritage and particularly for her work to preserve Wentworth Woodhouse. Julie's CBE in 2002 and honorary doctorate from Sheffield Hallam University in 2005 were conferred in recognition of her contribution to business in the region.

Julie has served as a deputy lieutenant for South Yorkshire since 2005 and was honoured to be the High Sheriff of South Yorkshire 2012/13. Julie was the Vitalise Businesswoman of the Year in 2013, Private Businesswoman of the Year 2014 and received a Special Recognition Judges' Award for Northern Power Women in 2018.

Julie has three grown-up children and had a successful career as a litigation lawyer in local authority and private practice before changing direction and founding Pyronix.

## Katy Leeson

Katy Leeson is a managing director of Social Chain UK, an IPA Woman of Tomorrow finalist, a public speaker, a LinkedIn Top Voice and a Campaign Female Frontier Awards honouree. Alongside this, Katy hosts her own chart-topping podcast, *I Shouldn't Say This, But*, which aims to confront taboo topics often avoided by managing directors. She shares her experience of being a woman in a predominantly male role, with guest appearances from business leaders from the world's best loved brands.

Social Chain is a global social media marketing agency working with some of the largest brands in the world, including Superdry, Arla, Coca-Cola and Boohoo. Katy's impressive career and accomplishments led her to secure the position of managing director after just six months at Social Chain. Not only has she secured a number of key retainers for the business, but a large proportion of her time is devoted to focusing on culture. Katy has implemented a number of policies at Social Chain that have allowed for the seamless expansion of the business and its culture across its five locations.

## Lara Morgan

Lara Morgan is a British entrepreneur whose investment strategy, primarily in wellbeing products, is committed to improving life's journey. She has a portfolio of six consumer services businesses, including Scentered.com, Kitbrix, Yogi Bare and Gate8. She is an inspirational but extraordinarily down-to-earth leader with a legacy of building world-class teams and aligning organisations against a clear strategy.

Lara is a philanthropist and active board member / advisor on various global non-profits. Annually, she sweats her way around Ride25 by bike for the 1morechild charity.

## Ayesha Nayyar

Ayesha is a renowned award-winning solicitor with over twenty years of experience in the legal field. In 2019 she was a winner in the Law Society's Excellence Awards, the Best Business Women Awards and the Asian English Awards. She was a presenter of the five-episode BBC series *Crime, Are We Tough Enough?* She has also made guest appearances on *BBC Breakfast*, *The Victoria Derbyshire Show*, *The Steph Show* and *Sky News*. She has written articles for numerous publications and blogs, and has a live call-in show on a local radio station.

Ayesha has her own law firm based in Manchester, which deals with various areas of law, including personal injury, family law, criminal injuries compensation and civil litigation. Ayesha is proud of her working-class heritage and being a Pakistani Muslim woman who is making strides in her industry.

## Linda Plant

 After leaving school at sixteen, Linda progressed quickly from selling fashion from a Leeds market stall to launching her international knitwear brand, Honeysuckle, which she sold for millions. After taking the company back, Linda later became one of the first women to head a fashion company flotation, with the business becoming a public limited company.

---

As a pioneer female business leader, Linda continued her business successes in a series of challenging executive roles, while consecutively growing and selling her electronics company for a substantial profit after just three years.

Linda is known as the 'Queen of Mean' for her no-nonsense interviews of the final five candidates of the BBC's *The Apprentice*, providing advice to Sir Alan Sugar over five seasons.

Linda's passion for business and entrepreneurship has also been recognised with a number of business awards and in her role as a judge for the top female entrepreneur for HSBC's Panel of Forward Ladies.

Today Linda runs the Linda Plant Business Academy, which empowers the next generation of business leaders, as well as her highly successful property development and interior design businesses.

Linda built her career from humble beginnings to become one of Britain's most successful business leaders. She now helps others to forge their own career path, through the Linda Plant Business Academy and Blueprint Business Course: www.lindaplant.com.

## Jacqueline de Rojas CBE

Jacqueline is the president of techUK, chair of Digital Leaders and co-chair of the Institute of Coding. She has held non-executive roles at Rightmove, Costain Group and FDM Group, and is a business advisor and mentor at Merryck.

Jacqueline is a passionate advocate for diversity and inclusion in all its forms. She works to redress the gender imbalance via advisory positions at the Youth Group, Accelerate-Her and Girlguiding.

In 2016 she entered the *Computer Weekly* Hall of Fame after being voted *Computer Weekly*'s Most Influential Woman in IT 2015. She was listed on Debrett's 2016 500 People of Influence and named in Europe's Inspiring Fifty most inspiring female role models for 2017. In 2017 she was presented with the Catherine Variety Award for Science and Technology.

In 2018 she received the Women in Tech Award for Advocate of the Year, acknowledging her contribution to diversity, and the #IB100 – most influential BAME leaders in tech. In 2019 she was awarded the Digital and Technology Award at the Asian Women of Achievement Awards, was included in the World's

100 most influential people in digital government, and was named Woman of the Year by Women in IT Excellence.

Jacqueline was honoured with a CBE for services to international trade in technology in the Queen's New Year Honours list 2018. You can listen to her life and music choices on the *Desert Island Discs* podcast, March 2019.

# The Author

As a former graduate recruiter at John Lewis and now working with a variety of employers and universities as managing director at graduate recruitment and employability consultancy SRS, Sophie Milliken is a recruitment and employability expert.

SRS is the leading provider of assessment centre simulations for universities, and Sophie and her team have trained over 30,000 students at these events. Sophie's passion to see every student and graduate being given the skills and knowledge they need to secure a fantastic job after university drives much of the work she does.

Sophie has been a Fellow of the Chartered Institute of Personnel and Development since 2013 and was awarded a Fellowship of the Royal Society of Arts in 2019.

A bestselling author, speaker and multi-award-winning entrepreneur, Sophie is passionate about helping others to excel and achieve their potential. Sophie is a huge supporter of women, acting as a mentor and coach, and is an active ambassador of Northern Power Women, Forward Ladies and City Ladies.

You can contact her via social media:

in www.linkedin.com/in/sophie-milliken

f www.facebook.com/SRSSophie

@SRS_Sophie

srs_sophie